Rhinos:
Conservation, Economics
and Trade-Offs

Michael 't Sas-Rolfes

Published by the
IEA Environment Unit

1995

First published in April 1995

by

THE ENVIRONMENT UNIT
THE INSTITUTE OF ECONOMIC AFFAIRS

2 Lord North Street, Westminster,
London SW1P 3LB

Studies on the Environment No. 4

All Rights Reserved

ISBN 0-255 36347-8

Cover design by David Lucas

Set in Plantin and Univers

Printed in Great Britain by
Goron Pro-Print Co Ltd, Lancing, W. Sussex

Table of Contents

Foreword .... *Frank Vorhies* 5

Preface .... *Roger Bate* 7

The Author 8

Acknowledgements 8

Introduction 9

1. **Background** 11
   The Historical Decline of Rhinos 11
   Human Use of Rhino Horn 12

2. **'Saving the Rhino'** 16
   Early Initiatives 16
   Efforts under CITES 18
   Field Conservation Measures 21
   The Funding Problem 22
   The Current Impasse 24

3. **Rhino Economics** 26
   Rhino Horn Is Different from Ivory 26
   The Ivory Ban's Initial Success 26
   The Long-Term Effects of Wildlife Trade Bans 27
   The Economics of Rhino Conservation 28
   The Economics of the Rhino Horn Trade Ban 32
      Significance of Price-Inelastic Demand 33
      Investment and Profit 34
   Future Demand for Rhino Horn 35
   Evaluating Alternatives 37
   Flooding the Market? 38
   Flawed Arguments Against Legal Trade 40

4. An Alternative Approach: Property Rights 43

    Whose Rhinos Are They Anyway? 43

    The Significance of Property Rights 43

    The Evolution of Property Rights 44

    The Problem: Misspecified Property Rights 46

    The Solution: Modifying Institutions 48

    A New Approach to Rhino Conservation Policy 50

5. The Future of Rhinos 51

    Scenario One: The Zoo Animal 51

    Scenario Two: The Ranch Animal 53

    The Most Likely Scenario 54

Appendix: A Suggested Bold Strategy for
             Rhino Conservation 58

List of Tables

    Table 1: Extant Rhinoceros Species and Subspecies, and
             Their Distribution in 1994 12

    Table 2: Some Recent Estimates of Wild
             Rhino Populations, 1981/82 to 1993 13

References/Bibliography 64

Summary .... *Back cover*

Foreword

CITES, the Convention on Trade in Endangered Species, is best known, ironically, for its efforts to stop the trade in endangered species. One such species is the African elephant. Another is the African rhino. There are hundreds of thousands of elephants and only tens of hundreds of rhinos. Nevertheless, at the recent CITES meeting in November 1994, limited trade in rhinos (live rhinos and trophies from South Africa) was sanctioned, while all trade in elephants remained banned.

In opening up limited trade in rhinos, CITES has accepted that some manner of trade may be beneficial to the conservation of endangered species. The challenge for CITES and indeed for the international conservation community is to understand how and when trade can be used to promote rather than hinder conservation.

The underlying challenge facing CITES is that trade bans now appear to have been an insufficient measure to reduce the economic incentives to supply and to demand wildlife products. The market for rhino products is a classic example of this problem. More than a decade of banned rhino trade has done little, if anything, to reduce the demand and only slightly more to reduce supply. Rhino products, in particular the horn, continue to be harvested in Africa for markets in the Middle East and Asia.

If stopping trade is not a viable option, then managing trade must be considered seriously. In this well-reasoned paper, Mike 't Sas-Rolfes carefully examines the benefits and costs of reopening the trade in rhino products. He further suggests a strategy for managing the opening of this trade to increase the probability that rhinos, as a wild species, will survive. This strategy addresses the important matter of existing stockpiles of rhino horn.

Readers inclined to support market solutions will be sympathetic to the line of reasoning developed here. They may, however, be doubtful of some of the specific proposals for institutional arrangements, such as cartels. These readers are asked to think carefully about the complexity of assigning property rights or use rights in a manner that preserves the wildness of the African rhino, while at the same time developing formal channels for trade in a species that has traditionally either been treated as common property or traded in illegal markets.

Readers sceptical of market solutions in general or the use of markets for managing endangered species in particular will be suspicious of, if not hostile to, the line of reasoning in this paper. They will need to make a special effort to set aside their preconceptions in order fully to appreciate the approach taken by 't Sas-Rolfes. It is not that their suspiciousness of markets for wildlife is unfounded. The ongoing illegal trade in rhinos may well lead to the extinction of rhinos in the wild. The issue here is whether the development of a legal trade in rhinos can improve matters.

Because of the political realities in much of Africa – endemic corruption, lack of transparency, lawlessness, civil unrest, and increasing pressures of population and poverty – a well-managed, legal trade in rhino products may not be possible. Illegal trade will nevertheless carry on. Thus the future for the African rhino is bleak. An attempt at managing a legal trade in this fragile continent may well be the only option before us to save the wild African rhino.

February 1995   FRANK VORHIES
                                                Resource Economist,
                         African Wildlife Foundation, Nairobi, Kenya

Dr Frank Vorhies *completed his doctorate in economics at the University of Colorado, USA, in 1982 and since then has been active in both academic and professional fields. He has published numerous academic articles and papers on wildlife conservation matters, and has consulted widely on environmental projects.*

Preface

The international ban on trade in rhino horn, in place for nearly 20 years, has not halted the decline of the five extant species of rhino. In this paper, Michael 't Sas-Rolfes explains that the attempts to stop trade mask the real issue, the lack of ownership of wildlife. 'Many environmental problems are a direct consequence of weak, non-existent or inappropriately allocated property rights.' (page 44)

Mr 't Sas-Rolfes not only criticises many of the present approaches to conservation, but takes the bold step of presenting a strategy for rhino protection. The IEA Environment Unit is delighted to offer this stimulating paper. The views expressed are of course those of the author, not of the Institute (which has no corporate view), its Trustees, Advisers or Directors.

February 1995   ROGER BATE
Director, IEA Environment Unit

7

The Author

Michael 't Sas-Rolfes was born in Belgium and raised in South Africa. He obtained his Bachelor of Commerce (Hons.) in Business Economics at the University of the Witwatersrand in South Africa, writing a dissertation entitled 'Privatising the Rhino Industry'. He consulted on the application of business economics to environmental problems for two years, before obtaining his MSc in Environmental and Resource Economics from University College, London. He has spent the last two years conducting economic research on rhino conservation and the illegal trade in rhino horn. His work includes numerous lectures, papers and articles on this subject.

He has been actively interested and involved in African wildlife conservation for over 15 years, conducting research and working with various conservation groups. After his work on rhinos, he is turning his attention to the issue of finance in the wildlife conservation sector, analysing potential economic returns and innovative ways to attract investment to African conservation and ecotourism developments. Currently based in Johannesburg, South Africa, he is a Fellow of the IEA's Environment Unit.

Acknowledgements

Because I have been working on the rhino issue for more than five years, it is impossible to name everybody who helped me over this period, but I would like to convey my sincere thanks to all. In particular, I would like to thank the three people without whose guidance my work would not have been possible: Frank Vorhies, David Pearce and Jorgen Thomsen. The World Wide Fund for Nature and Save the Rhino International provided valuable funding for some of my previous work, and I would like to thank them and the staff of TRAFFIC (Trade Records Analysis of Fauna and Flora in Commerce) for all their input and support.

I would like to thank Dan Leach, Wayne Safro and the two anonymous reviewers who commented on early drafts of this paper. I am also most grateful to John Blundell and the IEA staff for their support, and to my family and friends, especially Jean du Toit, for their support and understanding while I was working on the manuscript. Finally, I would like to acknowledge the considerable assistance of my two colleagues, Roger Bate and Julian Morris.

M.'t S.-R.

Introduction

There are many environmental issues that concern people nowadays, but few that can stir up as much public emotion as the perceived threats to 'endangered species'. Few people want to see *charismatic animals* like elephants, tigers, pandas and whales become extinct. As a result, 'saving endangered species' has become big business; there are countless non-profit organisations claiming to undertake this noble task, and raising considerable amounts of money in so doing. Sadly, the millions raised from well-meaning donors often fail to have much impact. The well-publicised issue of rhinoceros conservation is a typical example of this problem.

Most people who know something about rhinos believe that they are being rapidly hunted to extinction by greedy and ruthless poachers, in order to sell rhino horn to Asian people, who use it as an aphrodisiac. They also believe that to 'save the rhino', the trade in rhino horn must be stopped. Then, once again, rhinos could live undisturbed by humans. This view is seriously mistaken and uninformed. The whole issue of rhino conservation is far more complicated, and will require innovative and open-minded approaches, if any progress is to be made.

To understand the true nature of the forces driving rhino extinction, one has to be aware of the history of rhino exploitation, and the various recent attempts at rhino conservation – both the successes and the failures. Above all, one should understand the *economic* factors underlying the whole process, and how these determine the success or failure of conservation measures. Finally, one should realise that the underlying issue in rhino conservation is really one of 'ownership' or *property rights*. Understanding the rôle of property rights not only provides a far greater insight into the problem, but also helps to identify achievable solutions.

Unfortunately for some, there are no ideal solutions. The romantic notion that rhinos can one day roam completely wild and free is unrealistic. We can prevent rhino species from becoming extinct, but only by adopting certain bold measures, some of which are unpalatable to idealistic conservationists. Herein lies a major trade-off: we can either try to recreate a situation that we believe is perfectly 'natural' – and risk the extinction of one or more rhino species – or we can adopt a less purist approach, but one that is almost certainly safe (because it has already proven itself with many other species).

Sadly, the outlook for rhinos is a pessimistic one, because idealists currently outnumber pragmatists in conservation decision-making. However, there is some hope that if sufficient people are exposed to the facts, the tide of public opinion will turn in a more sensible direction. This paper has a somewhat unorthodox Appendix (pp. 58-63) – a proposed strategy to arrest the current decline of rhino populations, and ensure their successful conservation into the future. Readers are urged to consider all the issues discussed in the main text before passing judgement on the strategy. Thereafter, any constructive debate would be warmly welcomed.

1. Background

The Historical Decline of Rhinos

The extinction of rhinoceros species is not unique to present times. Fossil records show that in the past, at least 30 different rhino species roamed the Earth, on four different continents (Martin and Martin, 1982, p. 11). Most of these species disappeared in prehistoric times – during the Miocene, Pliocene and Pleistocene ages. Although climate changes probably led to the extinction of many rhino species, it is likely that humans have been at least partly responsible for the disappearance of rhinos for thousands of years. Evidence from a fossil site in central Germany shows that young rhinos constituted the major part of the diet of humans living there 80,000 years ago (Kyle, 1987, p. 8). Presumably these animals were among the easiest to hunt or trap for meat.

There are five extant rhinoceros species (Table 1). All are considered to be threatened with extinction from the wild. The decline in numbers of these animals during the last few centuries has been dramatic. Table 2 shows the most recent 'scientific' population estimates of each species. In the 19th century, the black rhino was the most abundant species, represented by at least several hundred thousand individuals, and as recently as 1960 there were thought to be about 100,000 left. Populations had been reduced to about 65,000 by 1970, and to 14,795 by 1980 ('t Sas-Rolfes, 1990, p. 4). By 1992 there were only an estimated 2,480 individuals remaining in the wild (African Rhino Specialist Group, 1992).

Two broad factors are responsible for the recent decline in rhino numbers: the disappearance of suitable habitat, and direct human exploitation. Humans have appropriated and converted rhino habitat for agricultural use, and they have hunted rhinos for their meat and various other products. There are documented uses for nearly all rhino body parts; these include the skin, bones, blood, fat, stomach, heart, penis, horns, hooves, teeth, eyes, tail hairs and even dung and urine (Martin and Martin, 1982; E. B. Martin, 1983). In recent years, the single greatest factor responsible for the rhino's demise has been the demand for rhino horn.

11

Table 1
Extant Rhinoceros Species and Subspecies, and Their Distribution in 1994

Black rhino *(Diceros bicornis)*
    Subspecies: Four
    Distribution: Angola*, Botswana, Cameroon, Ethiopia*, Kenya,
        Malawi, Mozambique, Namibia, Rwanda*, South
        Africa, Swaziland, Tanzania, Zambia & Zimbabwe.

White rhino *(Ceratotherium simun)*
    Subspecies: Two
    Distribution: Botswana, Kenya, Namibia, South Africa,
        Swaziland, Zambia & Zimbabwe (southern
        subspecies); Zaïre (northern subspecies).

Indian rhino *(Rhinoceros unicornis)*
    Distribution: India & Nepal

Javan rhino *(Rhinoceros sondaicus)*
    Subspecies: Two
    Distribution: Indonesia & Vietnam

Sumatran rhino *(Dicerorhinus sumatrensis)*
    Subspecies: Three*
    Distribution: Indonesia, Malaysia, Thailand*, Myanmar*,
        Vietnam† & Laos†.

Key: * Status uncertain   † Unconfirmed reports

Sources: Khan (1989); Cumming, du Toit and Stuart (1990); African Rhino
    Specialist Group (1994).

Human Use of Rhino Horn

A common fallacy, perpetuated by journalists, is that rhino horn is used mainly as an aphrodisiac. In fact, the two main uses of rhino horn are ornamental and medicinal. In the Middle East, rhino horn is used to make ornate dagger handles. In the Far East it is ground into powder form, and used as an ingredient in various traditional medicines for the treatment of colds, 'flus, fevers, headaches and other related ailments.[1]

The use of rhino horn dates back many centuries. An ancient Greek reference, dating from the fifth century BC, suggests that rhino horn was used to make drinking cups to detect

---

[1] It could be thought of as a traditional Chinese version of aspirin.

Table 2
Some Recent Estimates of Wild Rhino Populations

	Black rhino	White rhino	Indian rhino	Javan rhino	Sumatran rhino
1981/82	12,753	<3,561	1,500	50	?
1983/84	8,800	3,937	1,650	60	<600
1987	3,800	<4,658	1,893	50	<877
1993	2,550	6,784	<2,025	<100	<540

Sources: Martin and Martin (1982); E. B. Martin (1983); Cumming and Jackson (1984); Penny (1987); Cumming, du Toit and Stuart (1990); Milliken, Nowell and Thomsen (1993); African Rhino Specialist Group (1994).

poison[2] (Martin and Martin, 1982, p. 12). This practice was widespread until recent times. In addition to these functional vessels, cups and bowls were made for ornamental purposes, mainly by the Chinese. There are many examples of decorative vessels and other rhino horn carvings from the Tang, Sung, Ming and Ching dynasties, a period spanning the years AD 618 to 1912 (*ibid.*, pp. 53-54).

Some rhino horn was used for ornamental purposes in the 19th and early 20th centuries by Europeans, and there are also examples of African ornaments made of horn. In recent years, however, the predominant ornamental use has been in the Middle East, with Yemen being the largest market for rhino horn. Yemeni men wear traditional daggers called *janbiyyas* (Varisco, 1987, p. 25), which have ornate handles carved from a variety of substances. The most sought-after are those made with rhino horn. In ancient times, very few Yemenis had access to rhino horn, and antique examples of rhino-horn *janbiyya* handles have become extremely valuable.

During the 1970s, Yemen's economy experienced a sudden and dramatic boom, caused by a spillover of the surge in prosperity of neighbouring oil-rich Saudi Arabia. As a result, the demand for consumer goods in Yemen soared, with rhino-horn *janbiyyas* high on many people's wish-lists. In the 1980s and

---

[2] Many early poisons were strong alkaloids. Alkaloids probably react strongly with the keratin and gelatine in rhino horn, thereby indicating the presence of poison.

early 1990s, demand for rhino horn fluctuated somewhat, but before the outbreak of civil war in mid-1994, dealers were still willing to purchase it for about $1,200 a kilogram. Recent research by TRAFFIC[3] has revealed that rhino horn is also used to carve the handles of traditional daggers called *khanjars* in Oman, and that *janbiyyas* are also sold in the United Arab Emirates (CITES, 1994a, p. 1; 1994b, p. 7).

The use of rhino horn as an ingredient in traditional Chinese medicine dates back at least 2,000 years. Rhino horn is listed as one of 365 drugs in the *Shennong Bencao Jing* ('Divine Plowman's Herbal'), a reference in Chinese pharmacology written around 200 BC – AD 200 (But, Lung and Tam, 1988, p. 352). A later reference written in the 16th century, the *Pen Ts'ao Kang*, lists numerous ailments that can be treated with rhino horn (Martin and Martin, 1982, p. 68).

Proponents of Western medicine typically scoff at the idea that powdered rhino horn can be used for legitimate medicinal purposes, but recent scientific research has established that rhino horn has significant antipyretic (fever-reducing) effects when administered to rats with hypothermia (But, Lung and Tam, 1990, p. 157). Irrespective of its scientific validity, the belief that rhino horn medicines are effective is so well established that their use probably induces beneficial psychosomatic effects in many patients.

The Oriental trade in rhino horn has also existed for many centuries. The growing human population in China (and therefore increasing demand for medicines) probably led to the complete extinction of rhinos in that country by the 13th century AD (Martin and Martin, 1982, p. 89). As rhinos became increasingly scarce in China, the Chinese started to import horn, thereby placing other rhino populations in South-East Asia and Africa under pressure. As early as the second century AD, rhino horn was being exported from Africa to Arab and Indian ports, and by the eighth century, Arab traders were sailing to Cantonese ports with African horn.

Recent research by TRAFFIC and the Environmental Investigation Agency shows that Chinese medicines containing rhino horn are still sold in many countries.[4] The principal

---

[3] TRAFFIC (Trade Records Analysis of Fauna and Flora in Commerce) is a non-profit organisation that researches the trade in wild plant and animal products, especially those of endangered species.

[4] See, for example, Nowell, Chyi and Pei (1992), Mills (1993), Mulliken and Haywood (1994), and Environmental Investigation Agency (1994).

consuming nations are mainland China, Taiwan, Hong Kong and South Korea, although there are probably still markets in all Asian countries where Chinese people live. Manufactured medicines are also exported from China to North America, Europe and Oceania, wherever sizeable expatriate Chinese communities are found.

The horns of both African and Asian rhino species are used for Chinese medicine. In some markets, horn from Asian species (also known as 'fire horn') is considered much stronger than horn from African species ('water horn'). Consequently, Asian horn is far more expensive than African horn. According to a survey conducted in Taipei by Nowell, Chyi and Pei (1992, p. 14), the average wholesale price of African rhino horn in 1991 was US$3,075 per kilogram, while the wholesale price of Asian horn was US$60,025 per kilogram. Taiwan is one of the few markets where Asian horn is still consumed regularly; it is considered too expensive in other markets such as South Korea.

Research by TRAFFIC (Nowell, Chyi and Pei, 1992, pp. 22-23; Mills, 1993, pp. 18-20) shows clearly that the use of rhino horn in medicine will continue, despite attempts to criminalise it. The long tradition of use and fervent beliefs in its powers by many respected medical practitioners will ensure continued demand in traditional Chinese markets. Similarly, demand is likely to prevail in the Middle East. After conducting an in-depth anthropological study of the use of rhino horn in Yemen, Varisco (1987, p. 33) concluded that

'... the rhino horn dagger is so deeply a part of Yemeni culture, and a part still imbued with value as the country develops, that demand for it will not diminish simply because it is illegal to obtain it or to use it'.

The established traditional use of rhino horn and other rhino products by a large portion of the world's population cannot simply be ignored and wished away by Western conservationists. It is a factor that must be taken into full account when searching for a feasible solution to the current problem facing rhino conservation.

2. 'Saving the Rhino'

Early Initiatives

Since the early 20th century, there have been various initiatives to protect areas where wild rhino populations exist. However, the first concerted efforts directed specifically at conserving rhinos commenced in the early 1960s.

In 1961, the Natal Parks Board[5] launched 'Operation Rhino', an attempt to boost numbers of the rare southern white rhino. This subspecies had been reduced to a single population in the Hluhluwe/Umfolozi district of northern Natal, which numbered some 645 animals in 1960 (Martin and Martin, 1982, p. 124). Operation Rhino involved translocating large numbers of white rhinos to other reserves, private land and zoos. This bold initiative proved to be highly successful in creating new breeding nuclei. By 1987, the southern white rhino was the most abundant of all rhino species and subspecies. According to most recent estimates there were some 6,750 southern white rhinos in the wild[6] (African Rhino Specialist Group, 1994, p. 56), more than all the other remaining species and subspecies put together.

The year 1961 also saw the launch of the international conservation organisation, the World Wildlife Fund (WWF).[7] Its first public fund-raising campaign used rhino conservation as a central issue – including a photograph of a black rhino on the front page of the *Daily Mirror* (Bonner, 1993, p. 65). Subsequently, WWF donated money to field conservation projects, including support for the highly endangered population of Javan rhinos in the Udjung Kulong reserve in Indonesia. Unfortunately, budget constraints precluded donations to all field projects in need of funds, and consequently WWF could report only partial success. The black and Sumatran rhino species, and the northern race of the white rhino, continued to fare badly.

In the 1970s, the WWF and other conservation bodies focused

---

[5] The Natal Parks Board is a provincial conservation authority in South Africa.

[6] There were also 640 white rhinos in captivity.

[7] The WWF has changed its name to the World Wide Fund for Nature, although its US chapter still uses the original name.

attention on the trade in wildlife products as a threat to conservation, and in 1973, the United Nations' Convention on International Trade in Endangered Species (CITES) was formed. Twenty-one countries signed the original agreement, with the intention of regulating cross-border trade in certain plant and animal species and their products. By 1977, all five rhino species were listed on CITES Appendix I,[8] thereby prohibiting all commercial trade between signatory countries ('parties').

In the late 1970s, the WWF employed a geographer, Dr Esmond Bradley Martin, to research the markets for rhino horn in Asia. Martin established that rhino horn was used in the dagger handle and Chinese medicine trades, and dispelled the aphrodisiac myth. His research into the markets, which he has continued ever since, provided much valuable information. Unfortunately, however, almost all this information is of an anecdotal nature, and there are few reliable data on the rhino horn market.[9] It is thus impossible to track certain trends with any measure of confidence, especially as the market has gone underground during the last two decades.

Martin's early work showed that the demand for rhino products was extensive, deeply rooted in culture and tradition, and that prices had increased dramatically during the late 1970s (E. B. Martin, 1979; 1983). Despite this evidence indicating widespread and persistent demand, he suggested that 'ideally an immediate halt should be brought about to both poaching and

---

[8] Species listed on CITES Appendix I are supposed to be in danger of extinction (that is, 'endangered') according to CITES criteria; the convention allows no international commercial trade in these species and their products. Species that are less threatened are listed on CITES Appendix II, which allows regulated commercial trade only – that is, all transactions have to be approved by CITES.

[9] Most existing trade data are presented in Leader-Williams (1992). They are not presented in this paper because the author believes they would be more misleading than useful. There are at least four serious deficiencies with existing data. *First*, the data are not representative of the overall market. For example, the best data are from Japan, which accounts for an insignificant portion of the market, whereas there are almost no data from mainland China, a key consuming nation. *Second*, there are several possible distortions and inaccuracies in collected data because of the nature of the sources and collection methods. For example, official customs statistics may understate both the volumes and values of traded horn as there are strong incentives for traders to under-declare imports. *Third*, comparisons of data between countries are misleading. Not only do the markets in different nations vary greatly in their nature, but data were collected at different times using different methods – there are few, if any, consistencies between data sets. *Fourth*, because of the recent efforts to intensify trade restrictions, there are few reliable data for the last 10 years – arguably the most important period for analysing significant trends.

the trade in rhino products' (Martin and Martin, 1982, p. 115). This was the approach advocated by CITES, and one subsequently pursued with great vigour by nearly all leading conservation organisations, including the WWF.

In 1980, Dr Leslie Brown, a well-known Kenyan conservationist, suggested an alternative approach to the rhino poaching problem: to raise black and white rhinos for commercial harvesting. His idea was not well received. Other suggestions to remove the horns from live rhinos were not taken seriously (Martin and Martin, 1982, p. 123), although this approach would be adopted in Namibia and Zimbabwe less than a decade later (below, pp. 21-22).

Efforts under CITES

Throughout the 1980s, the CITES trade ban was promoted and intensified. At the third official CITES Conference of Parties (COP) in 1981, the parties passed a special resolution dealing specifically with the rhino horn trade. This resolution called on nations that were not parties to CITES also to take measures to prevent the international trade in rhino products, and it called for a moratorium on the sale of all government and 'parastatal'[10] stocks of rhino products.

The obvious failure of these measures to stem rhino poaching prompted a further resolution to be passed at the sixth CITES COP in 1987. This resolution called for more stringent measures, including the complete prohibition on trade in all rhino products and derivatives, both international *and domestic*. It also called for the *destruction* of government and parastatal stocks of rhino horn, and suggested that affected countries should be financially compensated for taking such action. Since the 1981 resolution was being ignored by governments of several countries, the new resolution recommended that parties should exert political, economic and diplomatic pressure on any countries that 'continued to allow the trade in rhino horn'.

The additional CITES resolutions were desperate attempts to give effect to the 1977 Appendix I listings, but were a clear indication of the failure of the trade ban policy. These resolutions exceeded the authority of the original convention by attempting

---

10 In this context, 'parastatal' refers to organisations that are not government departments, but operate as nominally autonomous public sector agencies. Many Parks Boards fit this description.

to pressurise non-parties to conform to CITES rules, and by attempting to dictate domestic trade regulations (being a convention on international trade, CITES has no official jurisdiction over the internal trade policies of its parties).

By the eighth CITES COP in 1992, no measurable progress had been made. Few official rhino horn stockpiles had been destroyed, and populations had been further reduced by poaching (below, p. 21). Dissatisfied with the performance of the CITES measures, two countries, South Africa and Zimbabwe, submitted proposals to 'down-list' their rhino populations to Appendix II, to allow controlled legal trade in rhino horn. Unfortunately, these countries also submitted proposals to down-list their elephant populations at the same meeting. At this time, a fierce debate was raging over the ivory trade issue, and the meeting was dominated by the presence of many vociferous environmental groups, lobbying aggressively against the elephant down-listing proposals. In the public eye, relaxing the trade bans on either ivory or rhino horn was sheer lunacy. Denied the opportunity to vote by secret ballot, CITES parties did not want to be seen to be voting for proposals perceived to be highly unpopular with the public. All down-listing proposals for elephants and rhinos were rejected.

The eighth CITES COP was followed by a period of intense efforts to implement the measures called for by the resolution passed in 1987. In 1992, the United Nations Environment Programme (UNEP) appointed Esmond Bradley Martin as a 'special envoy for rhinos', and provided him with funding to visit various countries to persuade their governments to abide by the CITES rules. Around the same time, the US Government yielded to pressure from environmental groups, and threatened wildlife trade sanctions against four rhino horn consumer nations, under the so-called 'Pelly Amendment'.[11] Governments of consumer nations responded to these pressures by passing some laws and intensifying efforts to control illegal trade, but these efforts only served to drive the trade further underground.

A notable feature of the early 1990s was the way in which opinions differed on the effectiveness of the CITES measures.

---

[11] The 'Pelly Amendment to the Fisherman's Protective Act of 1967' allows the US Secretary of the Interior to ask the US President to 'suspend any wildlife and fisheries trade between the USA and any country responsible for diminishing the effectiveness of an international treaty designed to protect threatened or endangered species' (Mills, 1993, p. 7).

Esmond Bradley Martin frequently cited successes, claiming that certain markets had been closed down and that prices were dropping, but was contradicted on several occasions. Research by TRAFFIC in Taiwan (Nowell, Chyi and Pei, 1992) and South Korea (Mills, 1993) found that both the prices and availability of rhino horn medicines were greater than had been previously claimed by Martin. An investigation into the export of manufactured medicines from the People's Republic of China (Mulliken and Haywood, 1994) also showed that rhino horn medicines were still being exported to several countries where Redmond and Martin (1992) were claiming that markets had been 'closed'. In 1991, Vigne and Martin claimed that Yemen was no longer a major buyer of rhino horn, but just over a year later, they reported another resurgence in imports (Vigne and Martin, 1992).

The initiatives of the early 1990s were fraught with political and practical problems, not to mention conflicts of interest. The US Pelly initiative clearly failed for these reasons — it was unable to bring about the closure of illegal markets in any of the four targeted countries. South Korea responded swiftly to the threat of sanctions by agreeing to become a signatory to CITES, and by performing a nationwide crackdown on pharmacies stocking rhino horn medicines. One pharmacist was arrested, and the authorities claimed that the rhino horn market was now closed. However, undercover research by TRAFFIC showed that not only were rhino horn medicines still widely traded on the black market, but also the retail price had doubled since the Pelly petition had been publicised in the local press (Mills, 1993, p. 16).

Taiwan, although eager to join CITES, could not do so because it is not recognised as a sovereign state by the United Nations. After a meeting in September 1993, the CITES standing committee had recommended to the USA that sanctions be declared against Taiwan and the People's Republic of China, because neither country had taken 'sufficient' action to eliminate its domestic trade in rhino horn. Six months later, President Clinton imposed sanctions against Taiwan, but not China. Indeed, a few weeks later he renewed China's 'Most Favoured Nation' trading status. Although Yemen's efforts to close down its market could also have been considered insufficient, invoking US trade sanctions in wildlife products would have been pointless – there is virtually no such trade between the USA and Yemen.

Field Conservation Measures

The 1987 CITES resolution had been passed at a time when one of the largest remaining wild rhino populations, the black rhino population of Zimbabwe's Zambezi Valley, was being subjected to intense poaching pressure. The resolutions had no positive effect on this situation – if anything, poaching intensified, despite the Zimbabwean wildlife department's policy to shoot poachers on sight (see Milliken, Nowell and Thomsen, 1993). By 1993, 167 poachers had been killed, 48 wounded, and 84 captured. Several rangers had also lost their lives, all to no avail. By late 1994 few, if any, black rhinos remained in the Zambezi Valley outside an Intensive Protection Zone (IPZ)[12] set up by the Zimbabwean wildlife department (Bridgland, 1994).

The Zimbabweans' attempts to protect their rhinos included not only the creation of IPZs, but also a comprehensive dehorning programme.[13] Namibian conservation authorities had already removed the horns from the black rhino population in the Damaraland region, apparently without seriously affecting the animals, so dehorning had gained some acceptance (see Milliken, Nowell and Thomsen, 1993, pp. 46-50). The Zimbabwean wildlife department removed the horns from animals of certain vulnerable populations, including the white rhinos of Hwange National Park. In early 1992, some 18 months after the dehorning programme started, the department experienced a serious shortage of funds, and was forced to cut back drastically on its anti-poaching patrols. During a three-month period, Hwange's white rhino population was almost completely wiped out.

Dehorning as an anti-poaching measure is the subject of some controversy. Those opposed to it argue that, aesthetic considerations aside, rhinos may need their horns for defence and other functions, and that losing them may be psychologically disturbing. Also, dehorning does not always deter poachers – several dehorned animals have been killed. There are various possible explanations for this.

○ *First*, it is only possible to remove about two-thirds of the animal's horn without harming it (the rest remains embedded

---

[12] An IPZ is a defined area designed to provide maximum security for rhinos.

[13] Dehorning is performed by darting the rhino to sedate it, sawing off the horns with a chainsaw, and then reviving it with an antidote. It is an intricate and expensive procedure, costing approximately US$1,000 per animal.

in the skull), so poachers may still find it lucrative to hack out the stump.

○ *Second*, the horn regrows fairly rapidly, so the deterrent effect wears off over time.

○ *Third*, poachers shooting rhinos in thick bush may not notice that they are hornless.

○ *Fourth*, a poacher who has tracked a rhino for several days only to find that it is hornless may shoot it anyway – either out of spite or to avoid wasting time tracking it again.

○ *Finally*, there is a conspiracy theory (based on the accounts of certain poachers arrested in Zimbabwe), that poachers are even paid to shoot dehorned rhinos, to help increase the value of accumulated illegal stockpiles of horn.

The Namibian and Zimbabwean conservation authorities have stockpiled horn from their dehorning operations and, along with South African and various other agencies, have also collected horn confiscated from poachers and recovered from dead animals. Consequently, there are considerable 'official' stockpiles of horn in the hands of government agencies, amounting to several tons, and worth millions of dollars. CITES regulations prevent this value from being realised, even if it were to be spent on rhino conservation.

The Funding Problem

Having experimented with various conventional and innovative protection measures, Zimbabwe's wildlife department could conclude that all these – including anti-poaching patrols, translocation, IPZs and dehorning – were extremely costly. The funds required for adequate protection of Zimbabwe's rhinos exceeded the department's entire annual budget. Zimbabwe is not alone. Most rhino range states[14] have underfunded wildlife departments. This issue was made clear at a meeting hosted by UNEP in Nairobi in mid-1993. At this meeting, governments requested US$60 million in *emergency* funds for rhino conservation for the next three years. Donor agencies pledged less than US$5 million over a period of 12 months, some of

---

[14] A 'range state' is any country in which rhino populations presently survive in their natural habitat.

22

which had already been previously allocated to other non-essential rhino conservation projects (Hurt, 1993).

While there was a serious shortfall of funds for field conservation, more money was being spent on law enforcement and underground intelligence. The South African Government created a new special branch of the police force, the Endangered Species Protection Unit (ESPU), to investigate poaching and illegal trade in species such as rhinos and elephants. Ash and 't Sas-Rolfes (forthcoming) note several instances during the early 1990s where the ESPU uncovered smuggling syndicates and arrested illegal dealers. A reputedly less successful initiative was 'Operation Lock', a project sponsored by the WWF with the support of Prince Bernhard of the Netherlands (*ibid.*; Bonner, 1993, pp. 78-81). Much secrecy surrounds this undercover attempt to break into smuggling rings, which collapsed in 1989 after its first phase.

Several important surveys were carried out by TRAFFIC, which provided crucial information on the ongoing trade. Some less methodical undercover work was also performed by members of the high-profile Environmental Investigation Agency. In 1993, they were able to film Chinese officials offering to sell over a ton of rhino horn, a month after China had claimed to have banned all rhino horn trade (Ash and 't Sas-Rolfes, forthcoming). In a recent initiative, six African countries signed the 'Lusaka Agreement on Co-operative Enforcement Operations Directed at International Illegal Trade in Wild Fauna and Flora' with the intention of improving co-operation between African law enforcement agencies (CITES, 1994a, p. 3). It is too early to see any effect of this initiative, which faces the potential obstacle of corruption within some enforcement agencies (see Bridgland, 1994).

At the ninth CITES COP (in November 1994), it was apparent that none of the initiatives adopted so far had been sufficient to end the trade in rhino horn. Furthermore, some of the measures called for in the 1987 resolutions were unrealistic. In particular, most parties steadfastly refused to destroy their stockpiles of horn, and few, if any, had been offered financial compensation to do so – indeed, there was a serious shortfall of rhino conservation funds. In its report entitled '[T]rade in rhinoceros specimens', the CITES Secretariat remarked that

'[T]he volume of government-held stocks has continued to grow, while poaching and illegal trafficking in rhinoceros horn have intensified' (CITES, 1994a, p. 1).

Recognising the shortcomings of the 1987 resolution, the

parties agreed to revoke it in favour of a more balanced approach. In particular, the request for the destruction of stockpiles was dropped. South Africa was also successful in achieving a down-listing to CITES Appendix II for its white rhino population, but subject to the condition that it would only trade in live animals and trophies. Despite these changes, however, the central objective of the CITES policy remained the same: to eliminate the trade in rhino products.

The Current Impasse

At the time of writing (early 1995), the trade in rhino horn is illegal within and between almost all countries, but still thriving underground. More important, rhino poaching continues and has recently intensified in South Africa, which now holds some of the last remaining sizeable populations of both African rhino species. The world's two largest white rhino populations (and two of the world's three largest black rhino populations) survive in South Africa's Hluhluwe-Umfolozi and Kruger National Parks. Both parks are surrounded by large communities of impoverished rural people, and both are close to Mozambique. The latter country, currently the world's poorest,[15] has just emerged from some 20 years of war. Mozambican nationals are desperately poor, but automatic weapons are widely available and inexpensive. Banditry and smuggling are on the increase. Drugs and arms are smuggled across the Swaziland and South African borders. With the current political changes in South Africa, and possible consequent disruptions in its conservation agencies, South Africa is surely ripe for a major onslaught against its rhino populations.[16]

South Africa, Namibia and Zimbabwe now harbour over 90 per cent of all the remaining rhinos in Africa, and at least 70 per cent of the global population. This amounts to around 88 per cent of the world's rhino horn on the hoof (measured by weight). All three countries have expressed interest in selling their stockpiles of rhino horn to procure much-needed funds for rhino

---

[15] According to the World Bank (1994, p. 162), Mozambique had the lowest GNP *per capita* in the world in 1992, at US$60. This is almost half that of the next poorest country, Ethiopia.

[16] In a recent press report, Bridgland and Neale (1994) allege that the latest official estimates of white rhino numbers in the Hluhluwe-Umfolozi park are overstated and that 800 rhinos have been 'lost', but this is refuted by the African Rhino Specialist Group (1995).

conservation. For the most part these countries also have institutions in place that would easily accommodate the resumption of legal trade – and ensure that funds were re-invested in conservation.

There is great resistance to any attempts to legalise the trade in rhino horn. Other African and Asian range states are strongly opposed to it, especially India, which has a policy of only allowing non-consumptive use of all wildlife. Many non-profit environmental groups also oppose legal trade, with several of their influential members arguing that the trade ban can be successful with more effort and more money (see Laurie, 1992; Lyster, 1992; and Redmond and Martin, 1992).

At the same time, other groups are starting to realise that existing efforts are unlikely ever to be successful, and are at least advocating investigation of more innovative approaches. One such organisation is TRAFFIC International (see Milliken, Nowell and Thomsen, 1993). Through its undercover work, TRAFFIC has observed the nature and extent of the market, and experienced increasing difficulty in monitoring illegal market activity.

At the 10th CITES COP to be held in early 1997, there is likely to be further debate on how best to tackle this continuing dilemma. How should it be approached? Essentially, there are two broad options – to continue with efforts to eliminate markets for rhino horn, or to accept the existence of these markets, and turn them to the rhino's advantage.[17] Which is the better option? To answer this question, the next chapter considers some economic issues underlying the whole problem.

---

[17] Some people have suggested that both options could be pursued simultaneously, but careful consideration of the implications of this proves that it is not really a feasible approach. If rhino horn is to be sold legally for profits to be re-invested in conservation, then the agencies selling it would want to achieve the highest possible prices for their stocks. It would hardly be in their interest simultaneously to discourage buyers and eliminate their potential markets.

3. Rhino Economics

Rhino Horn is Different from Ivory

When looking for solutions to the rhino conservation dilemma, many people are tempted to compare the rhino's situation to that of the African elephant. This comparison is not valid. Not only are the various rhino species far more endangered than the elephant,[18] but also the nature of the rhino horn market is very different from that of ivory. Furthermore, the ivory debate is clouded because elephants have to be killed to obtain their ivory. Rhino horn can be harvested from live rhinos without really harming them and it regrows, thereby enabling repeated harvesting at regular intervals.

The alleged effectiveness of the recent trade ban in ivory is also poorly understood. The ivory ban has been widely hailed as a conservation success, creating the belief that trade bans are an appropriate conservation tool. There are two reasons why this belief may be misguided. The first relates to the actual reason for the ban's initial success; the second relates to the long-term economic effect of any such trade ban (Barbier *et al.*, 1990, pp. 132-38; Sugg and Kreuter, 1994).

The Ivory Ban's Initial Success

As a short-term measure, there can be no doubt that the CITES ban on ivory trade and all the accompanying publicity had an immediate and substantial impact on the demand for worked ivory in Western markets.[19] Consumption of ivory in Western Europe and North America virtually ceased, thanks to an extensive and persuasive media campaign. In all probability, it was the media campaign that was so effective, and not enforcement of the ban. Western consumers stopped buying ivory because they believed that continuing to do so would

---

[18] With a remaining population of roughly 600,000, the African elephant does not even qualify for 'endangered' status under CITES Appendix I criteria (see Sugg and Kreuter, 1994, p. 35). Unlike the smaller remaining rhino populations, most elephant populations are free ranging – unprotected and unmanaged.

[19] These accounted for a shrinking, but significant, portion of the total demand. The largest consuming nations are Hong Kong, Japan and China. The ivory ban has had a mixed effect on consumption in these countries. (See Barbier *et al.*, 1990, p. 10.)

endanger the elephant, which they believed to be morally wrong. If they had not known or cared about the plight of the elephant, the ban would certainly have been far less effective. There is considerable evidence that the ivory trade continues (illegally) in most Asian markets, despite efforts to enforce the ban (see Dublin and Jachmann, 1992, p. 3; Dublin, Milliken and Barnes, 1995, p. 9).

In the longer term, the ivory ban may prove a less successful measure than initially appeared to be the case. Only part of the demand for ivory has disappeared, creating a temporary over-supply on the market. Although this glut initially led to a drastic drop in prices (and therefore a dramatic reduction in poaching in some areas), there are signs that prices are increasing again as surplus stocks are being used up. If some demand persists, and stockpiles are depleted, there is little doubt that illegal poaching and trade will again escalate.

The ivory ban's (short-term) success cannot be repeated for rhinos, for several reasons. *First,* the ban on rhino horn has been in place for much longer, and much stricter enforcement measures have already been adopted. Clearly, these have failed, and possibilities to improve their effectiveness are limited. *Second,* consumers of rhino horn differ markedly from the Western consumers of ivory. The latter viewed ivory as a luxury good, and had already made a partial cultural shift away from using other wild animal products such as spotted cat skins and furs (and rhino horn) for aesthetic purposes. Oriental consumers still frequently use wild animal products for food, medicinal and aesthetic purposes.

Unlike Western ivory consumers, those using rhino products usually know very little about the plight of rhino species, if indeed they are aware that these products even come from rhinos. Furthermore, if one considers that rhino horn medicines are used to cure some serious ailments, it is understandable that many consumers would place their lives and health before that of a strange animal in some distant land. To change the attitudes of rhino horn consumers will require much more than a simple media campaign (many consumers do not even have ready access to the media available to Westerners); it will require a complete change in culture. The probability of achieving this in the near future seems low.

The Long-Term Effects of Wildlife Trade Bans

In the long term, the bans on ivory and rhino horn may prove inappropriate for a more fundamental reason, which applies to bans on trade in products of most terrestrial animal and plant species. Elephants and rhinos compete with humans for space and resources. If we wish to conserve them, we need to forgo certain resources. Stated differently, we need to 'invest' resources in conservation. Without this investment, these animals will not survive. Typically, to justify any investment, investors seek some sort of return, even if this is non-pecuniary. The greater the return, the greater the amount that is likely to be invested (all other things being equal). If animals such as rhinos and elephants are perceived to provide small returns, little will be invested in conserving them.[20]

The long-term disadvantage of a trade ban is that it effectively lowers the value of the traded good relative to all others. Consequently, people will invest their resources in goods that yield higher returns. If African people can profit directly from cattle, but not elephants, why should they invest resources in elephants rather than cattle?

The trade ban approach also implies that conservation is costless, but that harvesting is costly, so to increase the cost of harvesting (by imposing criminal penalties) will be beneficial to conservation. This incorrect conclusion is reached when economic models of fishery management are applied to terrestrial species. Sugg and Kreuter (1994, pp. 46-48) discuss this issue in the context of the ivory ban. The following sections consider aspects relevant to rhino conservation.

The Economics of Rhino Conservation

The discipline of resource economics is increasingly being used as a tool to determine the optimal management of natural resources. Although early applications of resource economics focused strongly on optimal extraction of non-renewable resources, subsequent work has dealt with renewable resources in some detail, especially commodities of commercial interest such as timber and fish. The leading authority on this subject (known as 'bioeconomics') is Clark (1990), whose work consists largely of sophisticated fisheries models.

Swanson (1994) examines the extinction of terrestrial species. He argues that fisheries models are mistakenly applied to terrestrial species, leading to inappropriate policy conclusions. Most fisheries are open-access resources, and to prevent them

---

[20] For further discussion, see Barbier *et al.* (1990, pp. 11-29); Swanson (1994).

from being over-exploited, regulators attempt to increase the cost of harvesting. As the cost of harvesting is increased, so the rate of harvesting is slowed down. Fines for illegal fishing constitute an extra potential cost, and should slow down the harvesting rate. Consequently, the central policy of fishery regulation is to set renewable quotas, and use fines as a tool to ensure that these are not exceeded.

But fisheries differ fundamentally from terrestrial environments. Aquatic species do not compete with expanding human populations for land, whereas large animals like rhinos and elephants do. Furthermore, it is presently difficult, if not practically impossible, to apportion parcels of ocean or individual fish to private owners. On land, private ownership is far easier, and is a driving force behind economic development. Landowners are under constant pressure to achieve returns, and allocate resources accordingly, that is, they invest in the forms of land use likely to provide them with the greatest returns. If we treat rhinos and elephants like fish, and ignore the fact that they are competing for land with domestic animals, plantations and crops, we will undervalue them, and thus hasten their demise.

Most 'wild' rhino populations are found in reserves surrounded by poor rural people. In most cases, these people receive little or no benefit from either the reserves or the rhinos inside them. Consequently, they have few incentives to protect these rhinos, and may even want to see them vanish, so that they can occupy the land and use it for farming.

Swanson (*ibid.*, pp. 58-66) argues that an effective model for the management of terrestrial species must take account of two factors omitted by the Clark model: the allocation of base resources (natural habitat) and investment in management resources. After adding these components, 'the policy implications of the revised model are, for most species, diametrically opposed to those derived from the previous model'. Thus, whereas the Clark model suggests that the objective should be to place certain constraints on the profitability of harvesting, Swanson's model implies that profits should be *maximised*. Only by making wildlife management profitable will there be incentives to invest sufficient resources in conservation (provided that appropriate institutions are in place – see Chapter 4, below, pp. 48-50). Consequently, most policies that criminalise trade in wildlife products are probably misconceived.

Swanson's model certainly applies to the case of the Asian

rhino species, whose available habitat is under intense pressure from human encroachment and land conversion (Martin and Martin, 1982, p. 115). Also, in most Asian range states, considerable resources need to be spent on a continuing basis to protect rhino populations against poachers. In India and Nepal, some costs can be offset with income from tourism, but for countries protecting the forest-dwelling Javan and Sumatran species (which do not lend themselves to viewing by tourists), sources of income are limited. Consequently, effective protection of rhinos cannot take place without injecting large government subsidies. All Asian range states are developing nations, and most are reluctant to incur this cost.

In Africa, available habitat does not currently represent a constraint for rhino conservation. There are considerable areas containing suitable rhino habitat, where populations have been reduced or eliminated. The main constraint in African range states is investment in management resources. Milner-Gulland and Leader-Williams (1992a) discuss this issue in some detail, noting that few African countries can afford to invest sufficient funds for adequate protection of wildlife.

Research by Leader-Williams and Albon (1988, p. 535) shows clearly that the loss of black rhinos through poaching is inversely related to spending on management and protection. Modelling the incentives faced by poachers also shows that the most effective deterrent to poaching is to increase the probability of *detection*,[21] and that increasing penalties has a negligible effect if this probability is low ('t Sas-Rolfes, 1990, pp. 25-26; Milner-Gulland and Leader-Williams, 1992b).

This assertion is supported by analysis of poaching in Zimbabwe's Zambezi Valley between 1984 and 1993, where the effective penalty was frequently death ('t Sas-Rolfes, 1993, pp. 64-65). Clearly, the risk of death was insufficient to deter poachers, and since the penalty could arguably not have been increased, the only alternative was to increase the probability of detection. R. B. Martin (1991, p. 22) analysed available data on rhino population growth rates, poaching and deterrence in Zimbabwe. He concluded that, to contain poaching at a level where a positive population growth rate of 2 per cent could be

---

[21] This is equivalent to reducing the time taken to detect the presence of poachers (and intercept them *before* they reach and kill rhinos), as suggested by R. B. Martin (1991, p. 22).

achieved, the Zimbabwe wildlife department needed to spend US$20 million annually on protection. This sum amounted to almost double the amount the Government was allocating to the department.

An issue often highlighted in press reports is the relatively small reward poachers receive for their efforts. According to Milner-Gulland and Leader-Williams (1992b, pp. 399-400), Zambian poachers were being paid the local currency equivalent of roughly US$75 for a kilogram of horn in 1985. At this time, the wholesale price for African horn in Yemen exceeded US$1,000/kg, and retail prices in the Far East varied from about US$1,500 to US$18,700 (Leader-Williams, 1992, pp. 16, 26). Thus, according to these figures, poachers in Africa were receiving less than 7·5 per cent of the wholesale value (and between 0·4 and 5 per cent of the retail value) of African horn in Asian markets. E. B. Martin (1992, pp. 49-50) argues that Zambian poachers were actually receiving US$172/kg for horn during the early 1980s, which he claims was about one-third of the 'world market price', and that Kenyan poachers were receiving US$370/kg.[22]

While it is unclear which (if any) of these data are correct, there is a simple explanation for the evidence that poachers are willing to risk their lives for what may seem like a small return. The average annual income in Zambia is less than US$290 per annum, with the income of many people being well below that figure (many of them live at subsistence level), so that the prices paid to poachers are actually very attractive in relative terms (see 't Sas-Rolfes, 1993, pp. 64-65).

There are further strong incentives for smugglers and traders in Africa to deal in rhino horn, created by the fiscal and monetary policies of African governments (see E. B. Martin, 1992, pp. 48-49). Grossly overvalued local currencies and strict foreign exchange controls encourage considerable black market activity in many African countries. As a commodity with clear international value, rhino horn is sought after as a form of hard currency, and is very useful for smuggling value across borders in much the same way as diamonds.

---

[22] E. B. Martin (1983, p. 22) also claims that poachers in India were paid US$875 per Indian rhino horn in 1980, when the wholesale price ranged from $6,000/kg to $9,000/ kg. An average Indian rhino horn weighs about 720 grams, so this translates to a rate of about $1,200/kg, between 13 and 20 per cent of the wholesale value.

Rhino protection will remain a highly expensive activity as long as there is rural poverty in areas neighbouring reserves, and as long as inappropriate African institutions and government policies continue to create perverse incentives. By addressing these issues, some progress can be made (see Chapter 4, below, pp. 46-50). In the short term, however, there may be a far more serious threat: the CITES policy of banning the consumption of and trade in all rhino products. This issue is now considered in more detail.

The Economics of the Rhino Horn Trade Ban

There is considerable evidence that the demand for rhino horn is both extensive and persistent. After the CITES Appendix I listings in the mid-1970s, recorded wholesale prices and import values of rhino horn increased dramatically in several markets (see Leader-Williams, 1992, pp. 13-16). In Japan, recorded import values per kilogram increased from US$75 in 1976 to $308 in 1978; in South Korea they increased from $49 in 1976 to $355 in 1979 and $530 in 1981; in Taiwan they leapt from $17 in 1977 to $477 in 1980. In Yemen, the wholesale price of horn increased from $764 in 1980 to $1,159 in 1985.

These dramatic price increases indicate the persistence of the demand for rhino horn in the face of increasing restrictions on trade.[23] This is further supported by two more recent observations. First, according to E. B. Martin (1991), Chinese pharmaceutical companies have collected large quantities of valuable antique rhino horn carvings and bowls, with the intention of pulverising them to use in manufactured medicines. This suggests that, although the Chinese government has agreed to comply with CITES regulations on the import of new stocks of rhino horn, the market demand is sufficient to justify using up *all* existing stocks of horn within the country. The second observation is that by Mills (1993, p. 16), who found that the retail price of rhino horn in South Korea doubled with the imposition of stricter domestic measures in that country.

There is anecdotal evidence that in certain Asian markets, consumer demand for rhino horn is relatively insensitive to

---

[23] Prices increase because trade restrictions reduce the supply of horn to the market, but do not affect consumer demand to the same extent.

increases in price.[24] Technically speaking, the demand for rhino horn may be *price-inelastic* at present prices. This means that any percentage increase in price will cause a smaller percentage decrease in quantity demanded. There are many examples of goods for which demand displays such behaviour, including energy, water, alcohol, tobacco and various drugs.

Significance of Price-Inelastic Demand

The significance of price-inelastic demand is that it can render a ban unenforceable. A classic example of this was alcohol 'Prohibition' in the USA in the 1920s and early 1930s. During this period, consumption of alcohol was little affected but supply was constricted; thus prices soared on the black market (Thornton, 1991, pp. 103-10). Consequently, alcohol supply was so profitable that there were strong incentives for criminals to become involved in it. Not only did the alcohol business become dominated by organised crime, but there was considerable corruption in the government and the police force. Eventually, Prohibition had to be repealed, because it was too expensive to enforce and unpopular with the public. Similar patterns have been described in the market for illegal narcotics (Ostrowski, 1989), and as a result there is a growing lobby to legalise drugs.

In the case of rhino horn, not only is there much evidence of black market activity (such as the widespread continuation of rhino poaching for horn), but there are many instances in which government officials are implicated. According to press reports, those involved in illegal activity have included a senior ranger in the Kruger National Park, other parks employees, police officials, senior military officials, United Nations officials, Taiwanese and North Korean diplomats, a Zimbabwean Member of Parliament and even a Bhutanese princess.[25] In a recent report, Bridgland (1994) alleges the existence of a large smuggling syndicate, based in South Africa, and enjoying protection and co-operation from high levels of government in several countries.

The combination of possible price-inelastic demand for

---

[24] For example, many doctors claim that rhino horn has no substitutes as a medicine for treating certain ailments in Taiwan (Nowell, Chyi and Pei, 1992) and South Korea (Mills, 1993).

[25] This information is provided by Ash and 't Sas-Rolfes (forthcoming), who have collected and summarised press cuttings from local and national publications in African and other countries, containing information on poaching, illegal trade, arrests and convictions.

rhino horn and the reported high levels of corruption is cause for concern, because it suggests that not only is the ban unenforceable, but it may even encourage the rhino's demise. As long as demand remains price-inelastic, small reductions in the quantity supplied will result in large price increases. Under these conditions, anyone with monopoly power in the market can reap large profits. As Becker (1971, pp. 100-101) points out, the greater the inelasticity of demand, the greater the benefits from collusion. Under a trade ban, corrupt bureaucrats can effectively confer monopoly powers on certain illegal agents, by allowing them to operate while arresting other (competing) agents. If such powers are created, these monopolistic operators would probably stockpile horn to restrict the supply further, push up prices, and increase their profits. They would also have an incentive to encourage the destruction of legal stockpiles of horn, since this would constitute a further reduction in future supply, and would raise prices (and their profit margins) even further. With higher prices, the incentives for poaching would increase considerably.

Investment and Profit

It is also worth noting that the possibility that rhinos may become commercially extinct creates a unique potential profit opportunity for all holders of rhino horn stockpiles. According to resource economics theory, as an exhaustible resource (such as any mineral) is mined to depletion, its market price rises exponentially, until a point is reached where it is no longer viable to extract any more (Solow, 1974, p. 3). This level is known as the 'choke price', and is the point where commercial extinction takes place.[26] This mining model may apply to the extraction of rhino horn, since rhinos are being killed at a rate exceeding their rate of reproduction.

When considered together, the above factors have certain clear implications. If any individual or syndicate were able to control the supply of rhino horn, they could make extraordinarily large profits, which would be greatly enhanced by the commercial extinction of rhinos. Furthermore, if they had co-operation within government, they could use the ban to maintain monopoly power – enforcement agencies would clamp down on

---

[26] It is unlikely that illegal poaching will lead to the *complete* extinction of all rhinos, since a few will be inaccessible or too expensive for poachers to exploit. Whereas all wild populations may be eliminated, some animals will undoubtedly survive in zoos, ranches and intensively protected areas.

any competing operators. It is questionable whether any single operation possesses such power today, but there are indications that such a situation may develop. Many Zimbabwean conservationists already believe there is a conspiracy, and the recent information provided by Bridgland (1994) seems to support this view.

Even the prospect of gaining some monopoly power in the rhino horn market is sufficient to aggravate poaching. This is because rhino horn will be acquired and stockpiled for investment purposes. This investment demand will add to the demand from regular consumption, placing further upward pressure on the price.

What is so disturbing about the nature of this market, is that if large illegal operators enjoy government protection, they have an incentive to encourage the perpetuation of the ban, albeit for different reasons from those of idealistic conservationists.[27] Repealing the ban and allowing legal trade would simply create competition,[28] and could prevent the expected commercial extinction from which speculators are hoping to profit. Thus, as the rhino nears extinction, these operators could throw their weight behind the pro-ban lobby, campaigning side by side with those genuinely hoping to 'save the rhino'.

Future Demand for Rhino Horn

The above discussion assumes that underlying demand conditions for rhino horn remain constant. But what if those conditions change,[29] so that consumer demand declines relative to supply, causing a general drop in prices? In theory, with lower prices, the incentive for illegal activity would be reduced. In practice, two points are worth considering. *First*, with the already substantial profits being made by smugglers and other intermediaries, any short-term reduction in retail price is unlikely to have much effect. As long as poachers continue to accept relatively low compensation, and as long as the rhino's commercial extinction remains a probability, strong incentives

---

[27] In particular, they have an incentive to encourage the destruction of all official rhino horn stockpiles (as recommended by the 1987 CITES resolution) since this would greatly enhance their monopoly power.

[28] In a legal market, the entry of new legitimate suppliers would erode any monopoly profits being made by existing illegal suppliers.

[29] That is, the demand curve shifts.

for speculative buying will remain. *Second,* a dramatic reduction in wholesale prices would take place only if speculators expect future demand to drop at a rate that is proportionately much faster than the rate of rhino depletion. Otherwise, it may still be worth accumulating stocks now to release them onto the market after the rhino has become commercially extinct.

E. B. Martin (1993, p. 8) states that '[I]t is imperative that the price of rhino horn does not rise significantly in the next few years, as this would give poachers a greater economic incentive to kill more rhinos'. He then argues that demand for rhino horn 'must not be allowed to increase', and continues to claim that '[O]ne way of reducing demand is to eliminate the main markets left for rhino products'. In this context, 'eliminating' markets presumably means using CITES measures to criminalise market activity.

Martin's approach is decidedly optimistic. *First,* even if the wholesale price of horn does not rise, speculative stockpilers may be prepared to accept a lower 'mark-up' and pay poachers more, simply to acquire sufficient stocks before an expected commercial extinction. *Second,* as indicated above, a *drastic decrease* in both current and expected future demand is probably needed before any positive effect is felt on rhino poaching pressure. *Third,* the notion that criminalising markets will have sufficient impact on demand is questionable. The recent findings of TRAFFIC (and experience with other commodities such as alcohol and drugs) show that simply passing laws may not change consumer attitudes. Rhino horn is still regarded by many traditional doctors as an effective remedy.

Martin also points out that another way to reduce demand is to encourage the use of substitutes. He then goes on to recommend promoting the use of saiga antelope horn, having previously argued that '. . . this would not threaten their survival' (Martin and Martin, 1982, p. 128). This strategy, which was supported by the CITES standing committee, has encountered a setback: at the ninth CITES COP it was noted that saiga antelope populations are now under threat from illegal hunting, prompting a listing on CITES Appendix II.

But, Lung and Tam (1990, p. 157) assert that the horns of saiga antelope, water buffalo and cattle are effective substitutes for rhino horn, although the latter two need to be applied in much larger doses. While promoting the use of cow and buffalo horn seems a sensible approach, it may have limited success.

Nowell, Chyi and Pei (1992, p. 22) found that many Taiwanese doctors believe rhino horn to be 'irreplaceable', and a survey in South Korea revealed that 34 per cent of doctors believed that there was no substitute for rhino horn (Mills, 1993, p. 19).

Many other (sometimes frivolous) suggestions have been made to reduce demand for rhino horn, including the production of fakes, releasing poisoned horn supplies onto the market, and encouraging the use of Western medicines as a substitute. Apart from the questionable morality of certain suggested measures, none of these is likely to succeed, because of the way in which the traditional medicine market works (see Martin and Martin, 1982, pp. 127-28). Leader-Williams (1992, p. 36) points out that younger generations of Asians may reject traditional medicines and adopt conventional Western medicines, but there is no indication of the extent to which this may happen. It seems unlikely that any change in tastes will take place rapidly enough to prevent the depletion of further rhino populations.

It is also likely to be difficult to reduce demand for rhino horn in Middle Eastern markets. According to Varisco (1987, p. 23), rhino horn is by far the preferred component of dagger handles. The main reason for this is that rhino horn has some unique aesthetic properties that improve with age and handling (*ibid.*, p. 31).

Evaluating Alternatives

Faced with the prospects of continuing demand for rhino horn, possible perverse effects of the CITES measures, and the ongoing high costs of *in situ*[30] rhino protection, what is the most appropriate way forward? It is hardly possible to intensify the CITES measures, although individual consumer nations could probably spend more on enforcement. The problem is, they have little incentive to do so. Most consumer nations do not have their own rhino populations to protect, so by spending resources on enforcement they are effectively subsidising conservation in other countries.

Intensifying enforcement efforts is not only expensive but pointless if there are corrupt elements within enforcement agencies. With the considerable incentives for corruption, it is very unlikely that enforcement efforts can be completely effective. Furthermore, the use of certain enforcement strategies,

---

[30] *In situ* conservation refers to protection of rhino populations in their natural habitat. It is contrasted with *ex situ* conservation, which is the protection of rhinos under captivity.

such as 'sting' operations, may actually be counterproductive. Allowing enforcement agents to participate in black market activity not only increases the risk of corruption but may also stimulate poaching and other illegal activity that may not have previously taken place. 'Sting' operations may work as a smoke-screen, attracting new amateurs to the black market, while failing to harm the larger organised syndicates.

The only way the CITES approach can have any real effect is if underlying consumer demand is dramatically reduced in *all* markets. To achieve this will probably require a considerable investment in a well-planned education programme, designed to encourage all consumers to switch to substitutes. There is no indication of what such a campaign would entail to be successful, or how much it would cost, or who would be willing to pay for it. One cannot use the initial success of the ivory ban campaign as a precedent; the rhino horn market is larger in extent, and well-established in cultures that most Western conservationists know little about.

The only indication of what measures may be needed is provided by Varisco (1987, p. 41), who recommends that

'[C]oncerned conservation organisations and AID should not pursue the rhino horn issue in North Yemen apart from an overall effort in promoting wildlife conservation in the country'.

He goes on to suggest various measures, such as funding of conservation projects, establishing a zoo and national herbarium, and re-establishing herds of endangered ibexes and gazelles in protected areas. He provides no indication of how much such initiatives would cost.

Flooding the Market?

Given the probable lack of time and funds to bring about a change in cultural perceptions and attitudes, it is tempting to consider other possible short-term measures. One that is frequently discussed is 'flooding the market' with the official stockpiles of rhino horn. This would entail releasing large stocks of horn to cause a rapid and substantial drop in the price. There are at least three reasons why such a policy is inappropriate, and even dangerous.

First, there is likely to be considerable latent demand for rhino horn at lower prices. Many would-be consumers do not use rhino horn because of its high price, but would gladly do so if the price dropped.[31] Thus all the stocks of rhino horn could be absorbed by the market – and then what? Once these stocks were consumed, the price would return to even higher levels than before, with the knowledge that stockpiles had been further depleted. Poaching would resume and intensify.

Second, selling stocks at low prices may encourage further speculative buying by knowledgeable illegal operators who understand the short-term nature of this measure. After buying up all the cheap stocks they would command even greater monopoly power in the black market.

Third, this strategy would not allow conservation agencies to capture the value of the rhino horn stocks. A valuable opportunity to raise funds for conservation would have been squandered.

Attempting to manipulate or end the illegal trade in rhino horn does not appear to be a sensible policy. All possible measures are very costly, none guarantees success, and none directly addresses the core problem of unsustainable levels of rhino poaching. To reduce poaching, better protection of *in situ* populations is required. With sufficient investment in proven anti-poaching measures, it is possible to conserve rhinos effectively. But current funding levels are insufficient, and future costs are likely to increase further. Conservationists will have to find innovative ways to address the shortfall in funding for *in situ* conservation.

To reduce reliance on government subsidies and donor funds, several conservation agencies have already managed to raise considerable revenue from tourism. Whilst there are certainly many more opportunities for this approach, in some areas they are limited because of a lack of suitable infrastructure. In South Africa, trophy hunting of white rhino bulls generates considerable income for conservation agencies and private landowners,[32]

---

[31] This assertion appears to contradict the earlier argument that the demand for rhino horn appears to be price inelastic. However, it is quite possible, and even likely, that demand is inelastic at current price levels, but relatively elastic at much lower prices. This is because current market prices reflect the demand in the niche market for certain medicines that are regarded as having no substitutes. However, there are many other uses for rhino horn, and at low price levels people would probably start to buy horn for these various purposes; therefore the quantity demanded could increase considerably. (Technically speaking, market conditions could cause a point of inflection on the demand curve at low prices.)

[32] Properly managed, trophy hunting has little detrimental effect on rhino populations, since it is usually old non-breeding bulls that are shot.

and this activity can be expanded to other countries and permitted for the black rhino (for further discussion, see Milliken, Nowell and Thomsen, 1993, pp. 51-53). Such measures would help to raise further funds, but these may still be insufficient for effective rhino protection in all areas. The only remaining option is to consider allowing a controlled legal trade in rhino horn and other rhino products.

Flawed Arguments Against Legal Trade

Many arguments have been put forward as to why legal trade in rhino horn should not be attempted. While a few have some validity, most display considerable ignorance as to how markets function.

Comparing the illegal trade and exploitation of rhino horn to that of ivory, it is understandable that many people are reluctant to consider lifting the trade ban. However, there is a difference between the probable effects of lifting the ivory ban, and that of allowing a controlled legal trade in rhino horn. Most African elephants still survive in areas with almost no field protection from poachers. Many large populations live outside protected areas. Conversely, very few rhinos survive outside protected areas, and those that do are unlikely to survive for much longer.

If the ivory ban were lifted, poaching of unprotected populations would undoubtedly continue, since there are still hundreds of thousands of animals left, and very little incentive for most governments to invest in management. The situation with rhinos is different. Most surviving populations are carefully managed and protected. The few that are not could be translocated to safer areas. It is possible to implement a carefully planned conservation strategy if certain institutional reforms are brought into effect (see Chapter 4, below, pp. 48-50).

Since a legal trade in rhino horn would probably involve only the two African species, many conservationists are concerned about the possible detrimental effects it might have on Asian rhino conservation. There appears to be little reason for concern. African and Asian horns are readily distinguishable, so law enforcement should not be compromised if only trade in African horn is legalised. Also, Asian horns are not used in markets such as Yemen and South Korea, nor are they used in manufactured Chinese medicines, because of their prohibitively high price. African horn is clearly a substitute for Asian horn, and if it becomes relatively cheaper (as is most likely under legal trade), it is likely to replace Asian horn to a further extent in some markets. This should have the effect of reducing the demand for Asian horn, and thus lowering its price. An increased price leading to increased poaching is unlikely.

The most common misconception about the rhino horn trade is that 'the demand is too great for the supply' (Martin and Martin, 1982, p. 128), and it would therefore be impossible to satisfy the market if legal trade were introduced (Lyster, 1992). This argument is at odds with the most fundamental of economic axioms: the law of supply and demand. Basic principles of economics tell us that when the quantity demanded exceeds the quantity supplied at a given price, market prices tend to increase. When prices increase, the quantity demanded drops and the quantity supplied increases and a new equilibrium is reached. Thus demand cannot ever be 'too great for supply' as long as market forces are at work.

In the case of the rhino horn trade, the current suppliers are thieves, not the producers of horn. If the custodians of rhinos were allowed to enter the business of rhino horn production, they would respond to excess demand by raising prices, and investing profits in increasing future production capacity. Furthermore, they would not kill their animals, since this would be unnecessary; they would simply harvest horns on a regular basis. Some may argue that these producers would simply kill all their rhinos, sell the horns and retire with the proceeds. This argument is valid only if the discount rate[33] is extremely high (for example, when there is a very high perceived market risk), and is refuted by the considerable evidence of animal husbandry even under high risk conditions.[34] Farmers of cattle, sheep and other animals generally do not slaughter all their animals without ensuring the survival of some progeny.

The response to this (and most other arguments against legal trade) is that, provided market institutions are in place, a legal

---

[33] Discounting is the reverse of compounding, and is a technique used to equate present values with future values. For a full explanation see any basic text on environmental economics (for example, Pearce and Turner, 1990; Tietenberg, 1992) or finance (for example, Brealey and Myers, 1991).

[34] Poachers obviously have no incentive to husband the animals they poach, because these are not their property. Because of the considerable risks inherent in their profession, they face extremely high discount rates. Thus, poachers regard rhinos as an open-access resource (see Chapter 4, below, pp. 45-46), and in competing with one another, each has an incentive to kill as many rhinos as possible, and as quickly as possible.

trade in rhino horn should only *benefit* rhino conservation. The problem at present is that certain market institutions are lacking; in particular, there is a need to establish stronger property rights. I now consider this issue in more detail.

4. An Alternative Approach: Property Rights

Whose Rhinos Are They Anyway?

Throughout the previous chapter, the rhino conservation problem is considered as though all rhinos were the property of a single decision-maker. This is not the case. Some rhinos are owned publicly, some privately. Some people think that rhinos belong to them; some think that they should belong to everybody, and yet others think they should belong to nobody. If we consider the issue of *property rights* over rhinos, it not only provides a clearer understanding of the problem, but also leads closer to a practical solution.

Who presently owns rhinos? According to Swanson (1994, p. 149): '[F]or regulatory purposes, terrestrial natural resources are first and foremost national resources.' In reality, however, nations do not have an exclusive say over how to manage these resources. Certain environmental groups have, for example, used their lobbying power to influence CITES and governments of developed countries (such as the USA) to force other countries to accede to particular policies. In effect, these groups are attempting to claim ownership of rhinos.

Unfortunately for the environmental groups, *de facto* control over the destiny of rhinos vests in developing countries, with the managers of protected areas and their rural neighbours. In a sense, these people are the true 'owners' of rhinos. This state of affairs leads to considerable problems in effective decision-making. Environmental groups are frequently working at cross-purposes with people in the field, and governments are caught somewhere in the middle. Much time and money are wasted in the political battlefield trying to shape policies that are not implemented on the ground.

The Significance of Property Rights

Alchian (1987, p. 1,031) defines a property right as 'a socially enforced right to select uses of an economic good'. In this context, an 'economic good' can be thought of as any good or service that is relatively scarce and therefore has value. Rhinos can certainly be considered as economic goods, as can all other commercially valuable wildlife species.

'Ownership' is simply the placement with a person (or group of persons) of a certain group of rights to property: the rights of possession, use and disposal of worth (Harper, 1974, p. 18). As Alchian and Demsetz (1973, p. 17) note, a resource is incapable of being owned itself; it is only 'a bundle, or a portion, of rights to use a resource that is owned'. The strength of ownership 'can be defined by the extent to which the owner's decision to use the resource actually determines its use'. According to Alchian (1987, p. 1,031), the strength of a property right is measured 'by its probability and costs of enforcement which depend on the government, informal social actions, and prevailing ethical and moral norms'.

In recent years, economists have become increasingly aware of the importance of property rights, and the strong linkages between institutional structures and economic incentives. Seminal work in this area includes that of Coase (1960), Demsetz (1967) and Hardin (1968), and a survey of early work is provided by Furnbotn and Pejovich (1972). Not only are strong property rights important in determining incentive structures, but they are also an essential component of efficient markets, along with undistorted prices and unrestricted competition.[35]

Many environmental problems are a direct consequence of weak, non-existent, or inappropriately allocated property rights. Most welfare and environmental economists blame 'market failure' for environmental problems, but without clearly defined and enforced property rights, markets cannot function efficiently. Thus, 'market failure' is often a misnomer. When markets are absent or poorly developed, it is surely more accurate to speak of government failure or policy failure, since the definition and enforcement of property rights is one of the primary functions of government.

The Evolution of Property Rights

Much has been written about how property rights evolve. The 17th-century philosopher, John Locke, believed strongly in the virtues of private property, and discussed its evolution from 'the commons'. In recent years, economists have analysed this issue in detail. Hardin (1968) drew attention to the problems of

---

[35] For a further explanation of the rôle of the latter two factors, see Hayek (1948).

competitive open access to resources in his seminal article, 'The Tragedy of the Commons', which created the basis for much debate on the virtues of different resource management régimes.

In the literature there is some confusion over the term 'common property', since it is used to describe two distinctly different ownership régimes: open access and communal tenure. The issues discussed by Hardin relate mostly to resources to which there is unrestricted open access. In such cases, the incentive to over-exploit the resource is great, because the benefits of use accrue to a single person, whereas the costs are collectively shared. In the case of commercially valuable wildlife, each individual's rewards for harvesting are high compared with the rewards for conservation, which are dispersed across society.[36] However, not all communally-owned property suffers from this problem. There are many examples of successful sustainable resource management by traditional communal institutions (see Berkes, 1989; Ostrom, 1990). It is thus important to draw the distinction between cases where access is unregulated, and those where it is controlled, albeit by communal institutions (Bromley, 1991, p. 2). The effectiveness of such institutions depends on various factors, notably the 'population density' of the relevant community[37] (Krier, 1992, p. 337).

Historically, Western society has usually treated wildlife as an open-access resource, under the common law maxim of *res nullius*. According to this, any wild animal was considered unowned, until killed, captured or domesticated. As a result, wild animals had no value to individuals until they were 'converted' to dead, captive or tame animals. This had obvious disastrous consequences for wild populations of all species with commercial value. These consequences could be averted by creating property rights in live wildlife in its natural habitat. Such rights could be vested in the state, in local communities, or in private hands.

Demsetz (1967, pp. 351-53) describes the evolution of property rights in the fur trade. Before the trade became established, hunting 'could be practised freely'. However, the

---

[36] This phenomenon is referred to as 'rent dissipation' in resource economics literature (see Clark, 1990, p. 26).

[37] In general, communal institutions become less effective as the number of *residual claimants* increases (that is, the number of people who benefit from conserving the resource). The greater the number of residual claimants, the more dispersed the benefits of co-operation and the higher the costs of co-ordination.

advent of the trade had a significant impact on the value of the animals, and hunting increased rapidly as a result. This led to the delineation of private hunting areas, and the establishment of a seasonal allotment system. Eventually, the newly-created institutions encouraged the husbanding of fur-bearing animals, with hunting taking place on a sustainable basis.

Anderson and Hill (1975) further examine the evolution of property rights, and argue that the definition and enforcement of property rights will take place as it becomes economic to do so – that is, when the marginal benefits start to exceed the marginal costs. They then cite several historical examples from the USA, noting the crucial rôle of fences in establishing land rights. Another perspective is provided by Umbeck (1981) who emphasises the importance of force, both in determining the initial allocation of rights, and in maintaining their exclusivity. This observation is of particular importance in the context of many rhino range states, where a combination of force and corruption frequently determines the *de facto* allocation of property rights (for examples in Africa, see Ayittey, 1992).

Rhinos are typical examples of commercially valuable species that were treated as an open-access resource, and heavily hunted as a result (see Martin and Martin, 1982). However, despite the high commercial value of rhino products, the evolution of property rights has been much slower than that associated with fur-bearing animals. There are several possible reasons for this, mostly historical, which will not be discussed here. What is important is that stronger property rights régimes have recently developed in some countries (for instance, South Africa), while in other countries rhinos still effectively remain open-access resources. This differential between the stages of evolution of property rights régimes is related to the difference in attitudes of range states towards the rhino horn trade ban.[38] Countries with developed institutions are able to adapt to the conditions of legal trade and would benefit from it, whereas in countries without such institutions, legal trade may simply accelerate the rate of extinction.

The Problem: Misspecified Property Rights

The difficulty of achieving a sensible and co-ordinated strategy for effective rhino conservation is a direct consequence of the

---

[38] It is also one of the main causes of friction between countries over the ivory trade issue.

present institutions that govern decision-making in rhino management. Different decisions are taken by different parties and interest groups. The decision to harvest is taken by poachers, responding to forces of market demand for rhino products. The decision to allocate resources (land and management inputs) to conservation is made by governments, conservation agencies and private landowners in range states. Trade policy is decided by a complex political process, in which international environmental groups and governments from certain developed countries seem to have a disproportionate influence.

The detrimental effects of this diffused system of decision-making are exacerbated by the allocation of costs and benefits of rhino conservation. The benefits of harvesting accrue to poachers and illegal operators. The benefits of protection accrue largely to conservationists in developed countries. The costs of protection and losses through poaching are borne by the governments, agencies and citizens of developing countries. This problem, which is pervasive in biodiversity conservation issues, is discussed by Pearce and Moran (1994, pp. 17, 39-45), who term it 'global appropriation failure'. As they point out, international markets for biodiversity conservation are absent, and future international conservation initiatives should take this into account.

Many environmentalists seem to assume that wildlife belongs to everybody, a view that is implicitly supported by economists when they treat biodiversity as a 'global public good' (*ibid.*, p. 44; also see Swanson, 1994, pp. 19-44). In contrast, some radical environmentalists oppose the idea that humans can have any property rights over other life forms – this is the basis of 'animal rights' arguments (see Singer, 1976; Regan, 1980, 1983).

Should rhinos belong to everybody in the world? Or should they be considered as national property? Should individuals be allowed to 'own' them? Or should they have rights of their own, and therefore not be 'owned' by anybody, individually or collectively?

We can debate the moral and philosophical aspects of this issue at length, and never reach a satisfactory answer. However, if we are merely concerned with an effective means to conserve rhinos, economic analysis of past experience provides a clear answer. The answer is simply to vest strong property rights in the people or groups of people who have the greatest incentive to protect them.

47

The Solution: Modifying Institutions

This apparently simple theoretical solution encounters some considerable obstacles in the real world. Ideally, we should simply 'privatise' all rhinos – that is, we should vest full ownership rights in the individuals, communities, environmental groups and independent conservation agencies that have a genuine desire to conserve them. In practice, many governments and international organisations will resist this notion for ideological and political reasons.

We therefore need to seek 'second-best' solutions, based on the principle of establishing the most effective incentive structures. Here are some examples of such measures:

○ In countries where present institutions create an effective open-access régime, amend wildlife laws to allow stronger, more focused property rights over rhinos.

○ Where rhinos remain state property, ensure that the relevant government departments have complete autonomy over their finances and management decisions. If possible, create independent (i.e. parastatal) conservation agencies.

○ In communal areas, enable local communities to obtain direct economic benefits from activities related to rhino conservation.

○ Recognise the rôle of private landowners by allowing them at least some benefits from conserving rhinos on their land.

These are just a few examples of the options. Many conservationists are starting to understand the significance of economic incentives (see McNeely, 1989), which is resulting in the adoption of a variety of new and innovative strategies.

An approach that is popular with some economists is to use international institutions (such as the World Bank's Global Environment Facility) to transfer funds from developed to developing countries. The rationale for these transfers is 'global appropriation failure', and the objective is to create an artificial market for the 'existence value' of biodiversity (see Pearce and Moran, 1994, pp. 131-33). There are three potential disadvantages with approaches of this nature.

First, there is some difficulty in determining the appropriate value to be transferred. If 'existence value' forms the basis of the transfer, the only possible way to determine an amount is by using the Contingent Valuation Method (CVM). This entails using surveys to elicit people's personal opinions on value, and remains a controversial technique (see Bate, 1994).

Second, even assuming that the values to be transferred are derived appropriately, there is no guarantee that funds will be used effectively for their intended purpose, especially if they are donated to central state treasuries. A lack of strong property rights and effective institutions in many rhino range states is a serious obstacle to *any* initiatives conducted by governments. It is always preferable for funding to be transferred directly from individual donors to specific field conservation projects since this greatly reduces the risk of 'leakages'.[39]

Third, given the political realities of official donor funding, it is highly questionable whether funding through such mechanisms is sustainable. As long as rhino conservation remains a priority, donor funding may be helpful. But what happens when rhinos become unfashionable amongst those responsible for allocating funds? Self-funding local initiatives would seem to be a more sustainable approach.

There are countless case studies of initiatives that involve the effective devolution of property rights to local communities and private entities. Perhaps the best documented example is that of the 'CAMPFIRE'[40] programme in Zimbabwe (see Zimbabwe Trust, 1990). Although aspects of this project are frequently criticised, there is no doubt that it has had considerable success in involving local communities in effective wildlife conservation (for further discussion, see Sugg and Kreuter, 1994, pp. 51-56). The wide range of institutional models being adopted in various countries has led to many different two-way and three-way partnerships between government, local communities and the private sector. These form a potential basis for some interesting future empirical studies.

There is some concern that allowing complete private ownership of rhinos would lead to unsustainable harvesting practices. A case study from South Africa suggests that these fears are unfounded, so long as private owners are not provided with perverse incentives. A study by Buys (1988) suggested that

---

[39] 'Leakages' refers to money lost in the bureaucracy to administration, consultants, meetings, travel expenses, mismanagement of funds and other mostly unnecessary costs.

[40] Communal Areas Management Programme for Indigenous Resources.

the introduction of white rhinos onto private land had not been successful, because populations had been poorly managed, and had decreased in number. Closer examination revealed that many private landowners were simply purchasing rhinos from the Natal Parks Board for hunting purposes ('t Sas-Rolfes, 1990, pp. 9, 32-33). Since the Parks Board price was heavily subsidised, landowners could make an instant gross profit of up to 600 per cent by selling the animals as trophies. When the Parks Board stopped supplying rhinos at subsidised prices, and started to auction them instead, the average market price of a live animal increased to about 50 times the original subsidised price! Trophy fees also increased, but not to the same extent (*ibid.*, p. 37). With a true market price established for live rhinos, more private owners started husbanding their animals, and management improved dramatically.

A New Approach to Rhino Conservation Policy

Possibly the most appropriate approach to rhino conservation policy would be to allow a range of competing institutional models, and to monitor their performance. If strong property rights were defined and recognised, and CITES restrictions on consumptive use of rhino products were eased, the owners of rhino populations would determine an appropriate mix between the demands for consumptive and non-consumptive uses of rhinos. Since rhino owners would have to bear the consequences of their own actions (that is, bear the direct economic costs of any losses), they would have a strong incentive to manage their populations efficiently.

As there is undoubtedly a substantial demand for rhinos to be used non-consumptively (most tourists prefer to see live rhinos with their horns intact), some landowners would accommodate this market. Others would supply the product markets, and by doing so would ease some of the pressure on the unharvested populations. The advantage of this arrangement would be that market forces would determine a mixed and balanced approach to rhino conservation. This would be a vast improvement on the current situation, in which those wanting to use rhino products are fighting preservationists[41] in the political arena, and both are likely to end up losing.

---

[41] In this context, a 'preservationist' is someone who wants to save each and every individual of a species, whereas a 'conservationist' would accept the sacrifice of some individuals to save the whole species from extinction.

5. The Future of Rhinos

As rhinos approach their eleventh hour, the range of possible solutions to the poaching problem is becoming limited. Essentially, there are only two broad options: to intensify measures under the approach currently adopted by CITES, or to implement a radical change in policy. Depending on which approach is adopted, one of two scenarios is likely to take place. Neither scenario is ideal for those wanting a return to former times when rhinos could roam in the wilderness, undisturbed by humans. 'Saving the rhino' will necessarily entail a trade-off.

Scenario One: The Zoo Animal

If the CITES policy of a complete ban on trade is not revoked within the next few years, three things are likely to happen. *First*, since it seems unlikely that demand for rhino horn will disappear, poaching and illegal trade will continue. The rate at which this will take place depends very much on expected future demand and price trends, but unless the underlying demand for horn drops substantially, prices are likely to increase as stocks diminish.

With the long-term prospect of increasing prices, some illegal operators may decide to stockpile horn as an investment, thereby adding to current demand for fresh supplies of horn. The high profits to be made in the illegal trade will also provide an incentive for corruption. Illegal operators may work with corrupt government officials to gain monopoly power in the rhino horn market. As they acquire such power, they will have a stronger incentive to gain an even larger market share, and may attempt to drive the rhino close to extinction, to enhance the future value of their stocks. They may, therefore, offer increasing rewards to rhino poachers.

Second, rhino conservation *in situ* will become increasingly costly. Unless *per capita* income in rhino range states increases (which is currently not happening in most cases), rising rhino horn prices and rural poverty will create even greater incentives for poaching, and conservation agencies will need to spend even more resources on anti-poaching measures. Partly because of declining national income, law enforcement budgets are actually

51

decreasing in many African countries (Dublin and Jachmann, 1992, p. 1; Dublin, Milliken and Barnes, 1995), and it is doubtful whether this trend will be reversed.

The three largest remaining African rhino populations (in Namibia and South Africa) are likely to be subjected to intense poaching pressure. The factors that could bring this about are all in place: rural poverty in neighbouring areas, availability of cheap automatic weapons, established smuggling routes, and continued foreign exchange controls in South Africa. Such an onslaught could also happen very quickly, taking authorities by surprise.[42] If the last large rhino populations are lost, conservation departments will incur additional expenses as they translocate isolated animals to safe areas, and move animals around to ensure exchange of genetic material (to prevent inbreeding in small populations).

Third, the first two factors will probably lead to a situation in which African countries translocate many of their rhinos to overseas sanctuaries, and protect remaining animals in small intensive protection zones (this trend is already evident in countries such as Kenya and Zimbabwe). Rhinos will only survive in areas with strong security measures, far away from poor people. Few will remain in their natural habitat, and the African rhino may effectively become a zoo animal.

In Asia, costs of protection are also likely to increase, and some populations (especially of the Sumatran rhino) are unlikely to withstand the increasing poaching pressure. If sufficient funds are spent on intensive protection (as is currently taking place in Kaziranga in India), and this is maintained, some Asian rhinos stand a chance of surviving in the wild. However, the long-term outlook for *in situ* protection of Asian rhinos seems fairly bleak. Projected costs of Asian rhino conservation are estimated to be some US$57·5 million over the next five years, and US$33 million will be sought from 'external' sources over the next three years (African Rhino Specialist Group, 1994, Appendix II). What are the chances that these funds will be provided, and is it realistic to expect external donors to fund rhino conservation in Asian countries on an ongoing basis?

---

[42] There are many precedents for this – for example, the sudden disappearance of the key Zimbabwe populations in the early 1990s, and the elimination of nearly 3,000 rhinos in the Central African Republic in the space of just two years (E. B. Martin, 1992, p. 49).

Scenario Two: The Ranch Animal

As indicated in the previous chapter, it would make little sense to revoke the CITES policy unless certain institutional changes preceded this move. However, if property rights were strengthened, then it would be a logical step to remove the barriers to legal trade in rhino products. With the right incentive structures in place, many conservation agencies and private landowners would decide to harvest horns from live animals selectively, and sell them for a profit. In most instances, these profits would be re-invested in management.

With strong property rights, harvesting of animals for other products would take place on a sustainable basis, except in conditions of extreme political instability (there are probably no measures that can effectively protect rhinos under such conditions). As with any other form of animal husbandry, harvesting would be done in a way that ensured the replenishment of stock.

Not all rhinos would be husbanded for the horn and products markets. The demands of tourists and environmentalists would ensure that some rhinos remain in natural conditions in protected areas. Although dehorning of animals in national parks and game reserves would probably be used as an initial precautionary measure, some of these animals would eventually be allowed to live with minimal human interference.[43]

The Appendix to this paper (below, pp. 58-63) outlines a possible bold strategy to achieve the conditions described under this scenario. While these conditions may not seem ideal to senti-mental conservationists, preservationists and animal rights activists, they represent the best chance to prevent the first scenario from becoming a reality. Allowing ranching and controlled legal trade in rhino products will certainly ensure that more money is invested in protecting rhinos, which in turn will ensure that more rhinos survive.

There are many precedents for the type of ranching and controlled management régimes described here. There are obvious examples of large mammals with commercial value that are husbanded and ranched under free-range conditions such as cattle, sheep and goats, but there are also many less known examples of 'wild' animals being successfully used in this way. For example, in southern Africa, several different antelope

---

[43] They would obviously require continued protection from poachers.

species are ranched to supply the growing venison market. This development has not been prejudicial to these species; on the contrary, numbers of these animals are increasing considerably.

Ostriches and crocodiles are two examples of animals that yield products of high commercial value, and that are farmed or ranched on a large scale; wild populations of these animals continue to exist in many places, without being materially affected by this activity. In South America, the vicuna, a previously endangered species, is now used commercially to its advantage (see Thomson, 1992, pp. 186-87). Highly prized for their wool, wild vicunas are captured, sheared and released periodically. Again, this policy appears to have been beneficial to the species. Further examples include the farming of deer in New Zealand to supply deer horn to the Chinese medicine market, and the private ranching of previously endangered bison (wild buffalo) in North America.[44]

The Most Likely Scenario

Which of the above two scenarios is more likely to take place in the next few years? By analysing the incentives of those controlling the rhino's destiny, one reaches the sobering conclusion that the first scenario is the more likely.

Consider the parties that are likely to gain, and those that are likely to lose, if the CITES trade ban is revoked and the bold strategy is adopted. The 'winners' would include the following:

o *Rhino range states*: Rhino conservation would eventually cost these countries far less than it does now, and rhinos would be an asset for attracting tourists.

o *Bona fide conservationists*:[45] These people would have the satisfaction of knowing that rhinos are no longer threatened with extinction, and may be enjoyed by future generations.

o *Consumers of rhino products*: All consumers of rhino horn and

---

[44] There is a common misconception that rhinos are somehow different from all these other species, because the costs of rhino ranching seem prohibitive, or because it seems difficult to establish individual private ownership in the field. Such arguments are completely unfounded and incorrect.

[45] In contrast to preservationists and animal rightists, true conservationists would be genuinely committed to seeing rhinos conserved in their natural habitat according to the principles of 'sustainable living' (see IUCN/UNEP/WWF, 1991).

other rhino products could purchase these freely, legally and probably at lower prices.

○ *Conservation agencies*: By selling their stocks of rhino horn, parks and wildlife agencies would not only earn more funds to protect their rhino populations, but benefits would also spill over to other species and habitat conservation; the increased profitability of protected areas would also help to stem land encroachment pressure from neighbouring communities of poor rural people.

○ *Rural communities*: Poor rural people would benefit in some areas, as shares of the profits were passed down to them.

○ *Taxpayers*: Taxpayers in many countries ought to benefit indirectly as governments stop wasting money on ineffective law enforcement measures; further gains should be felt in the developed countries whose governments currently fund ineffective rhino conservation initiatives.

○ *Donors to 'Save the Rhino' campaigns*: Members of environmental groups, and those donating to special rhino conservation funds, could spend their money differently.[46] For example, they could focus on supporting specific field preservation schemes, or they could spend their money on 'ecotourism' holidays, thereby contributing to the continued economic prosperity of conservation projects.

○ *Rhinos*: Arguably, most rhinos would benefit from this approach. First, more individual rhinos and rhino species would survive. Second, their quality of life would probably be improved; instead of being poached (sometimes by very cruel methods such as snaring), they could be harvested more humanely. Furthermore, they could roam in their natural habitat, rather than live under captive or intensively protected conditions.

The 'losers' under this approach can be classed into three main categories:

○ *Criminals*: Since a legal trade would render illegal activity less

---

[46] A considerable amount of the money donated to 'save rhinos' is currently spent on administration, meetings, publicity campaigns and other activities that are of no direct benefit to rhinos.

profitable, all poachers, smugglers, illegal dealers and corrupt bureaucrats would lose income.

○ *Bureaucrats and politicians*: Government officials who have made a career out of the creation of legislation or law enforcement activity may have to look for new occupations. Also, some proponents of trade bans may lose credibility.

○ *Environmental groups*: Many non-profit environmental organisations raise considerable funds from campaigns to 'save rhinos'. Their fund-raising campaigns would be seriously affected by the adoption of such an approach for two reasons: first, because many of their donors would be alienated by a bold approach to conservation, and second, because if the approach were successful, they would lose their rationale for fund-raising.[47] Radical environmentalists (such as animal rights advocates) may feel that their principles have been compromised.

Although the 'winners' appear to outnumber the 'losers', the latter are likely to be far more influential in deciding the direction of future policy. This is because CITES policy is determined largely by the actions of environmental groups and certain influential bureaucrats. The strong lobby of preservationists and animal rightists can argue for trade bans with impunity. They do not bear the costs of their actions; nor are these borne by the bureaucrats who vote for CITES resolutions – the costs are borne by people in the rhino range states.

Sadly, even environmental groups with more pragmatic attitudes towards conservation may be reluctant to embrace bold strategies. This is because they rely heavily on sentimental and poorly informed members of the public for donations. Changing the perceptions of these members is costly and complicated, so such groups prefer to tread lightly when it comes to sensitive issues. A classic example of this is the WWF's reticence on the subject of sustainable consumptive use of wildlife.

Despite the pessimistic tone of this conclusion, there is still some hope that conservationists will start to adopt a more flexible approach to this issue. At the most recent CITES

---

[47] This does not mean that all environmental groups have sinister motives. Many of them would be quite happy to lose donor funding if they were able to achieve one of their stated objectives. Unfortunately, some of them do have strong disincentives to be *too* successful in achieving these objectives too quickly.

Conference of Parties there was evident dissatisfaction with the performance of trade bans, not only for rhinos, but for the conservation of many other species too. Perhaps by the next CITES meeting, conservationists will have given serious thought to some critical economic issues; in particular, they may have considered the long-term viability of donor-funded field conservation in the face of increasing pressures for land and consumption of animal products. Hopefully, they will also have considered the importance of property rights, and the way in which these may be modified to the advantage of wild species.

It is not too late to adopt a bold approach to the *in situ* conservation of rhinos. But there is not much time left for dallying.

Appendix

A Suggested Bold Strategy for Rhino Conservation

The current objectives of different rhino conservationists are varied, extremely complex and often contradictory. All may agree that they would not like to see rhinos become extinct, but they may disagree considerably on what comprises an ideal situation (for example, what is the optimum size and population density of a genetically healthy population?).

Ignoring the more intricate issues, let us consider three main objectives (which are almost universally acceptable to conservationists). In order of importance they are:

(1) To conserve genetically viable populations[1] of each individual species 'in the wild' – that is, in their natural habitat.

(2) To conserve genetically viable populations of each subspecies in their natural habitat.

(3) To minimise human interference with, or disturbance of, wild rhino populations.

For rhino populations to qualify as being 'wild' (non-captive), three conditions must be satisfied:

○ They must be free-ranging within an area large enough to sustain a breeding group.

○ The area in question must consist of natural rhino habitat.

○ They must survive by feeding off the natural vegetation in the area (that is, without human intervention).

The following is a suggested outline of a course of action to reverse the decline of wild rhino populations, and achieve the above objectives. It entails setting up appropriate institutions and phasing in a controlled legal trade in rhino horn. Being an outline only, this strategy cannot pretend to be comprehensive, and many intricate details have been omitted. Nevertheless, this

---

[1] Most conservationists seem to favour a minimum total population of 2,000 animals (see Khan, 1989, and Cumming, du Toit and Stuart, 1990).

should not detract from the overall nature and expected effect of the strategy.

In chronological order, the following steps could be taken:

1. Establish Appropriate Institutions

This first step is an absolutely vital prerequisite for any legalisation of trade. It would entail changing national wildlife laws governing property rights over rhinos. The aim is to create conditions under which almost all rhinos are owned and/or controlled by private, communal or autonomous public institutions, with appropriate incentive structures in place. This framework is necessary to ensure that all custodians of rhinos (private and public) are provided with an incentive to invest in adequate protection.

Where rhinos are found on private land, the private landowner should be entitled either to complete ownership, or (where state-owned rhinos have been moved temporarily to private land for safety reasons), to a significant portion of any profits derived from the future sale of rhino products.[2] Where rhinos are owned communally, care should be taken to ensure that the number of residual claimants is not so large as to undermine the incentives for co-operative management. Where rhinos are owned publicly, the relevant agencies should at least be allowed full financial autonomy – that is, they should possess and control their own funds, and not simply operate through the national treasury. This is essential to ensure that funds earned from rhinos are re-invested in rhino protection and conservation measures, and are not lost.[3]

If certain range states with small, insignificant populations refuse to effect the necessary institutional changes, they should not be allowed to obstruct the implementation of the strategy. Those nations unwilling to co-operate for ideological or other reasons should reap the consequences of their policies, without imposing them on other nations.

2. Consolidate All Remaining Rhino Populations

Conservation agencies and private landowners should consolidate and secure all rhino populations under their jurisdiction. Small

---

[2] Certain countries (such as South Africa) already recognise wildlife ranching as a legitimate form of enterprise, and have passed laws allowing private landowners to benefit directly from ownership of wildlife.

[3] Some conservation agencies (for example, the Parks Boards in South Africa) already have this autonomy, and it has clearly added strength to their effectiveness.

isolated groups in remote areas should be captured and translocated to safe locations (well-protected reserves and sanctuaries), or those where larger protected populations already exist.[4] Populations still considered vulnerable should be dehorned routinely, with the horn being stored in secure locations. Where possible, funding for intensive protection, translocation and dehorning could be obtained by borrowing against future projected earnings from the sale of horn.

3. Establish a Protocol for the Sale of Rhino Horn

Once relevant laws and institutions are in place and all rhino populations are relatively secure, it would be necessary to establish a protocol for any legal sales of horn, to ensure that all countries co-ordinate their activities. This step is important to ensure that the initial legal suppliers to the market are not out-manoeuvred by powerful illegal operators, and would probably be necessary to obtain CITES approval of the strategy.

The exact form that such a protocol would take, should be considered carefully. At first, it may be desirable to create a tightly controlled market structure for selling horn. One such option would be to form a multinational cartel, similar to the de Beers Central Selling Organisation which markets diamonds. The structure of this organisation would ensure initial control over supply to the market. Shares in such an organisation could be allocated to all significant rhino conservation agencies, private and public, if they satisfy certain institutional requirements (that is, if the structures are in place to ensure that any profits are re-invested directly into rhino conservation).

However, a cartel structure has some distinct disadvantages, and should only ever be considered as a short-term option. By being able to restrict supply, cartels can push up market prices. If abused, this monopoly power can encourage illegal competition (and thus a return to the original problem of rhino poaching). Within a cartel there are also strong incentives for cheating and corruption. The advantages of such a structure would necessarily only last for an initial period.

The whole question of establishing the right structure for a protocol is one that needs to be researched in great detail and considered very carefully before implementation.

---

4 See Thomson (1992, pp. 132-42) for a more detailed discussion.

4. Consolidate All Stockpiles of Rhino Horn

All agencies possessing rhino horn should consolidate, weigh, and register their stockpiles. They should pledge a proportion of their stocks for an initial sale, in accordance with the protocol, to receive a share of profits from the first sale of horn. The agencies pledging their horn stocks may need to allocate some funds to agencies that are unable to supply horn, but have pressing conservation funding needs.[5]

Note: Certain consumer countries (such as The People's Republic of China) also have large official stockpiles of horn. Ideally, these countries should also either pledge their stocks, or contribute funds to range states with pressing needs.

5. With CITES Approval, Publicly Announce the Intention to Sell Horn

Having established all the appropriate structures and secured all rhino populations and horn stockpiles, the next step would be to obtain CITES approval to commence legal trading under Appendix II (the legal trade proposal should satisfy all CITES criteria). Initially, all international transactions would need to be approved according to the protocol; no other bodies would be authorised to issue CITES permits. Besides the CITES down-listing, certain countries would need to revoke laws preventing domestic trade or consumption of rhino horn products.

The first sale of horn should be preceded by a public announcement of the clear intention to establish controlled legal trade on a continuing basis. This move would discourage further accumulation of stockpiles by illegal operators.

6. Sell a Small Percentage of Existing Stockpiles

The most appropriate way to commence legal trade would be through a public auction system. This would facilitate the early determination of the true market value of horn. Initially, agencies should sell only a small proportion (say, 10 per cent) of available stocks to avoid flooding the market and pushing the price too

---

[5] For example, African agencies may need to contribute some funds to agencies in Asian range states, since the latter would probably be unwilling or unable to supply horn stocks. Initially, the African agencies should accept this situation, because they will be unable to sell any horn without the co-operation of the Asian agencies.

low (after all, their primary objective is to obtain profits to re-invest in rhino conservation).[6]

By this stage, the steps taken will have had a definite effect on the illegal market. It is impossible to predict exactly what would happen, although it would be reasonable to expect at least a noticeable fall in the market price of horn in wholesale markets. In any event, it does not matter much what happens to the price of rhino horn. Consider each of the following cases:

(a) The price remains at high levels

In the unlikely event that wholesale prices do not fall,[7] range states could face increased poaching pressure. However, the high prices would enable them to make large profits, which they could then use to fund increased anti-poaching measures.

If, after repeated sales of legal stockpiles, the price of horn remains high, rhino conservation will continue as a highly intensive activity. This would probably lead to development of sophisticated rhino ranching projects, which would evolve more efficient techniques to supply the market. Rhinos retained in reserves for tourist viewing would need to be closely monitored and protected.

(b) The price falls drastically

If the price of rhino horn falls sharply to very low levels, this may be for one of two reasons: either illegal stockpilers have panicked and dumped their stocks, or the black market was previously poorly informed as to the real scarcity value of horn. The second scenario is unlikely. If stockpilers do dump their stocks, further legal sales of horn would have to be carefully managed, because prices could increase again over time as these stocks are used up. However, having retained most of their stocks, agencies would be equipped to deal with possible future increases in demand.

If the price remains very low into the long term, conservation agencies will be unable to profit much from the sale of horn. However, they will also save money on enforcement expenditure because the incentive for rhino poaching will certainly have been reduced. Rhino populations would be safe, except in marginal areas.

---

6 Flooding the market is also dangerous, because it could allow illegal stockpilers to snap up large supplies of horn at bargain prices, and regain control of supply.

7 It would be even more surprising if prices were to increase. This would only happen as a response to extraordinary market conditions.

(c) The price falls marginally

If the price falls somewhat, but not sufficiently to cause a marked reduction in poaching pressure, agencies would need to re-invest profits from the legal horn sales into protection. Periodic sales would eventually result in a stable price being reached. By this time, agencies and landowners will have determined the optimal levels of harvesting and enforcement expenditure to enable continued effective conservation of rhino populations.

References/Bibliography

African Rhino Specialist Group (ARSG) (1992): Proceedings of the meeting of the African Rhino Specialist Group held at Victoria Falls, Zimbabwe, 17-22 November 1992. Pietermaritzburg: IUCN Species Survival Commission.

—— (1994): Proceedings of the meeting of the African Rhino Specialist Group held at Mombasa, Kenya, 23-27 May 1994. Pietermaritzburg: IUCN Species Survival Commission.

—— (1995): 'White Rhino in Hluhluwe-Umfolozi Park, South Africa: Have 800 Been "Lost"?', Key Issue Report No. 1, Pietermaritzburg: IUCN Species Survival Commission.

Alchian, A. A. (1987): 'Property Rights', in John Eatwell, Murray Milgate and Peter Newman (eds.), *The New Palgrave Dictionary of Economics*, London: Macmillan, pp. 1,031-34.

Alchian, A. A. and H. Demsetz (1973): 'The Property Rights Paradigm', *Journal of Economic History*, Vol. 33, pp. 16-27.

Anderson, Terry L. and Peter J. Hill (1975): 'The Evolution of Property Rights: A Study of the American West', *Journal of Law and Economics*, April, pp. 163-79.

Ash, P.K. and M. J. 't Sas-Rolfes (forthcoming), *Rhinos in the Press*.

Ayittey, G. B. N. (1992): *Africa Betrayed*, New York: St. Martin's Press.

Barbier, Edward B., Joanne C. Burgess, Timothy M. Swanson and David W. Pearce (1990): *Elephants, Economics and Ivory*, London: Earthscan.

Bate, R. N. (1994): *Pick a Number: A Critique of the Contingent Valuation Methodology and its Application in Public Policy*, Washington DC: Competitive Enterprise Institute.

Becker, Gary S. (1971): *Economic Theory*, New York: Alfred A. Knopf.

Berkes, Fikret (ed.) (1989): *Common Property Resources: Ecology and Community-Based Sustainable Development*, London: Belhaven Press.

Bonner, R. (1993): *At the Hand of Man: Peril and Hope for Africa's Wildlife*, London: Simon & Schuster.

Brealey, R. A. and S. C. Myers (1991): *Principles of Corporate Finance*, 4th Edn., New York: McGraw-Hill.

Bridgland, F. (1994): 'The end of the rhino', *Sunday Telegraph Review*, 11 December 1994, pp. 1-2.

Bridgland, F. and G. Neale (1994): 'How South Africa "lost" 800 white rhinos', *Sunday Telegraph*, 11 December 1994, p. 1.

Bromley, D. W. (1991): *Environment and Economy: Property Rights and Public Policy*, Oxford: Basil Blackwell.

But, P. P-H., L-C. Lung, and Y-T. Tam (1988): 'Profiles of Chinese Medicines. 4: Rhinoceros horn', *Abstracts of Chinese Medicines*, Vol. 2(3), pp. 351-60.

—— (1990): 'Ethnopharmacology of rhinoceros horn. 1: Antipyretic effects of rhinoceros horn and other animal horns', *Journal of Ethnopharmacology*, Vol. 30, pp. 157-68.

Buys, D. (1988): 'A Summary of the Introduction of White Rhino onto Private Land in the Republic of South Africa', Bedfordview, Republic of South Africa: Rhino and Elephant Foundation.

CITES (1994a): 'Trade in Rhinoceros Specimens', *Proceedings of the Ninth Meeting of the Conference of the Parties in Fort Lauderdale, United States of America*, Doc. 9.28, 7-18 November 1994.

—— (1994b): 'Conservation of Rhinoceros in Asia and Africa', *Proceedings of the Ninth Meeting of the Conference of the Parties in Fort Lauderdale, United States of America*, Doc. 9.35, 7-18 November 1994.

Clark, Colin W. (1990): *Mathematical Bioeconomics: The Optimal Management of Renewable Resources*, 2nd Edn., New York: Wiley-Interscience.

Coase, R. H. (1960): 'The Problem of Social Cost', *Journal of Law and Economics*, Vol. 3, pp. 1-44.

Cumming, D. H. M. and P. Jackson (1984): *The Status and Conservation of Africa's Elephants and Rhinos*, Gland: IUCN.

Cumming, D. H. M., R. F. du Toit and S. N. Stuart (1990): *African*

Elephants and Rhinos : Status Survey and Conservation Action Plan, Gland: IUCN.

Demsetz, H. (1967): 'Toward a Theory of Property Rights', *American Economic Review, Papers and Proceedings*, Vol. 57, pp. 347-59.

Dublin, H. T. and H. Jachmann (1992): *The Impact of the Ivory Ban on Illegal Hunting of Elephants in Six Range States in Africa*, Gland: WWF.

Dublin, H. T., T. Milliken and R. F. W. Barnes (1995): *Four Years After the CITES Ban: Illegal Killing of Elephants, Ivory Trade and Stockpiles*, Gland: IUCN.

Environmental Investigation Agency (1994): *CITES enforcement not extinction*, London: EIA.

Furnbotn, E. G. and S. Pejovich (1972): 'Property Rights and Economic Theory: A Survey of Recent Literature', *Journal of Economic Literature*, Vol. 10, pp. 1,137-62.

Hardin, G. (1968): 'The Tragedy of the Commons', *Science*, Vol. 62, 13 December, pp. 1,243-48.

Harper, F. A. (1974): 'Property in its primary form', in S. L. Blumenfeld (ed.), *Property in a Humane Economy*, LaSalle, Illinois: Open Court, pp. 1-22.

Hayek, F. A. (1948): *Individualism and Economic Order*, South Bend, Indiana: Gateway Editions.

Hurt, Leigh Ann (1993): 'Funding falls short in bid to save the world's rhinos', press release from World Wide Fund for Nature, 2 July, Gland.

IUCN/UNEP/WWF (1991): *Caring for the Earth: A Strategy for Sustainable Living*, Gland, Switzerland: IUCN/UNEP/WWF.

Khan, Mohd. Khan bin Momin (1989): *Asian Rhinos: An Action Plan for their Conservation*, Gland: IUCN.

Krier, James E. (1992): 'The Tragedy of the Commons, Part Two', *The Harvard Journal of Law and Public Policy*, Vol. 15 (2), pp. 325-48.

Kyle, R. (1987): *A Feast in the Wild*, Oxford: KUDU Publishing.

Laurie, Andrew (1992): 'The Rhinos of the World', in Kristin Nowell, Wei-Lien Chyi and Chia-Jai Pei (eds.), *Workshop on a*

Programme to Control Taiwan's Trade in Rhino Horn: Proceedings, Taipei: TRAFFIC, pp. 4-12.

Leader-Williams, N. (1992): *The World Trade in Rhino Horn: A Review*, Cambridge: TRAFFIC.

Leader-Williams, N. and S. D. Albon (1988): 'Allocation of resources for conservation', *Nature*, Vol. 336, pp. 533-35.

Lyster, Simon (1992): 'On the horns of a dilemma', *WWF News*, Winter.

Martin, C. B. and E. B. Martin (1982): *Run Rhino Run*, London: Chatto and Windus.

Martin, E. B. (1979): *The International Trade in Rhinoceros Products*, Gland: IUCN/WWF.

―― (1983): *Rhino Exploitation – The Trade in Rhino Products in India, Indonesia, Malaysia, Burma, Japan and South Korea*, Hong Kong: WWF.

―― (1991): 'Rhino Horn in China: A Problem for Conservation and the World of Art', *Wildlife Conservation*, Vol. 94(1), pp. 24-25.

―― (1992): 'Africa's Rhino Horn Trade from 1970 to 1985: An Economic Explanation', *Kenya Past & Present*, pp. 48-52.

―― (1993): 'The present-day trade routes and markets for rhinoceros products', *Rhinoceros Biology and Conservation: Proceedings of the International Rhino Conference in San Diego, United States of America*, 9-11 May 1991.

Martin, R. B. (1991): 'Rhino Population Dynamics, Illegal Hunting and Law Enforcement in the Lower Zambezi Valley in Zimbabwe', paper presented at the International Symposium on the Biology and Conservation of Rhinos, San Diego, California, 9-11 May, 1991.

McNeely, Jeffrey A. (1989): *Economics and Biological Diversity*, Gland: IUCN.

Milliken, Tom, Kristen Nowell and Jorgen B. Thomsen (1993): *The Decline of the Black Rhino in Zimbabwe : Implications for Future Rhino Conservation*, Cambridge: TRAFFIC.

Mills, J. A. (1993): *Market Under Cover: The Rhinoceros Horn Trade in South Korea*, Cambridge: TRAFFIC.

Milner-Gulland, E. J. and N. Leader-Williams (1992a): 'Illegal Exploitation of Wildlife', in Timothy M. Swanson and Edward B. Barbier (eds.), *Economics of the Wild*, London: Earthscan Publications.

—— (1992b): 'A Model of Incentives for the Illegal Exploitation of Black Rhinos and Elephants: Poaching Pays in Luangwa Valley, Zambia', *Journal of Applied Ecology*, Vol. 29, pp. 388-401.

Mulliken, Teresa and Mandy Haywood (1994): 'Recent Data on Trade in Rhino and Tiger Products, 1988-1992', *TRAFFIC Bulletin*, Vol. 14/(3), pp. 99-106.

Nowell, Kristin, Wei-Lien Chyi and Chia-Jai Pei (1992): *The Horns of a Dilemma: The Market for Rhino Horn in Taiwan*, Cambridge: TRAFFIC.

Ostrom, E. (1990): *Governing the Commons*, Cambridge: Cambridge University Press.

Ostrowski, J. (1989): 'Thinking About Drug Legalization', *Policy Analysis*, No. 121, Washington DC: Cato Institute, 25 May.

Pearce, David W. and Dominic Moran (1994): *The Economic Value of Biodiversity*, London: Earthscan.

Pearce, David W. and R. Kerry Turner (1990): *Economics of Natural Resources and the Environment*, Baltimore: Johns Hopkins University Press.

Penny, M. (1987): *Rhinos: Endangered Species*, London: Christopher Helm.

Redmond, Ian and E. B. Martin (1992): 'Don't Argue – Save the Rhino', *BBC Wildlife*, November, p. 44.

Regan, T. (1980): 'Utilitarianism, Vegetarianism, and Animal Rights', *Philosophy and Public Affairs*, Vol. 9(4), Summer.

—— (1983): *The Case for Animal Rights*, London: Routledge.

Singer, Peter (1976): *Animal Liberation*, London: Cape.

Solow, Robert M. (1974): 'The Economics of Resources or the Resources of Economics', *American Economic Review, Papers and Proceedings*, Vol. 64, pp. 1-14.

Sugg, I. C. and U. P. Kreuter (1994): *Elephants and Ivory: Lessons from the Trade Ban*, IEA Studies on the Environment No. 2, London: IEA Environment Unit.

Swanson, Timothy M. (1994): *The International Regulation of Extinction*, London: Macmillan.

Thomson, R. (1992): *The Wildlife Game*, Westville, South Africa: Nyala Publications Trust.

Thornton, M. (1991): *The Economics of Prohibition*, Salt Lake City: University of Utah Press.

Tietenberg, T. (1992): *Environmental and Natural Resource Economics*, 3rd Edn., New York: Harper Collins.

't Sas-Rolfes, Michael J. (1990): 'Privatising the Rhino Industry', Free Market Foundation Paper, No. 900501, Johannesburg: Free Market Foundation.

—— (1993): 'The Economics of Rhino Conservation', Master's dissertation, University College, London, July 1993.

Umbeck, John (1981): 'Might makes rights: A theory of the formation and initial distribution of Property Rights', *Economic Enquiry*, Vol. XIX, January, pp. 38-59.

Varisco, D. M. (1987): *Horns and Hilts – Wildlife Trade in North Yemen (YAR)*, a report prepared for Asia/Near East Bureau Agency for International Development, Washington, DC, under a co-operative agreement with WWF/US Project 6298, unpublished.

Vigne, L. and E. B. Martin (1991): 'Yemen Stops Being a Major Buyer of Rhino Horn', *Pachyderm*, Vol. 14, pp. 20-21.

—— (1992): 'Upsurge of Rhino Horn Imports into Yemen', *Endangered Wildlife*, Vol. 12, pp. 3-6.

World Bank (1994): *World Development Report 1994*, New York: Oxford University Press.

Zimbabwe Trust (1990): *People, wildlife and natural resources – the CAMPFIRE approach to rural development in Zimbabwe*, Harare: Zimbabwe Trust.

Global Warming: Apocalypse or Hot Air?

Roger Bate and Julian Morris

1. The greenhouse effect is real – without it none of us would be alive.

2. The enhanced greenhouse effect – or 'global warming' – is contestable science, with as yet little empirical support.

3. Some warming of the Earth's atmosphere may have occurred over the past 100 years, though most of the observed change occurred before 1940.

4. Atmospheric concentrations of carbon dioxide and other greenhouse gases (GHGs) have approximately doubled since 1850, but most of that increase occurred after 1940.

5. Rising levels of carbon dioxide may well be beneficial. Crop yields should increase and water requirements fall. (Good news for those living in arid places.)

6. Uncertainty should make us more rather than less wary of imposing limits on emissions of GHGs.

7. Carbon taxes and subsidies to energy efficiency are both unnecessary and inefficient.

8. Most research into the social and economic costs of global warming is futile since neither costs nor benefits can be estimated.

9. Government funded research into climatology and geoengineering crowds out private investment and encourages a false consensus.

10. All energy subsidies and taxes should be eliminated – the market and its supporting institutions will then be able to adapt more readily and rapidly to a changing environment.

IEA Studies on the Environment No. 1

Institute of Economic Affairs
2 Lord North Street
London SW1P 3LB

Telephone: (0171) 799 3745
Facsimile: (0171) 799 2137

£5.50 inc. p + p

ISBN 0-255 36331-1

Elephants and Ivory:
Lessons from the Trade Ban

Ike C. Sugg and Urs P. Kreuter

1. The African elephant is not an endangered species: there are at least 10 viable populations.

2. The UN Convention on International Trade in Endangered Species (CITES) broke its own rules by listing the African elephant as endangered.

3. The international trade ban, instigated by CITES, was opposed by 73 per cent of those countries with elephant populations.

4. Southern African countries argue that allowing trade maximises the value of elephants.

5. Prior to the ban, the elephant populations in Botswana, South Africa and Zimbabwe had increased with the assistance of protection made possible by tourism and the sale of hunting licences and elephant products.

6. Banning the use of elephant products reduces the value of the elephant by denying financial benefit to the elephant's custodians.

7. Kenya banned hunting in 1976. Since then, it has lost 85 per cent of its elephants.

8. Zimbabwe granted land-owners title to their wildlife in 1975; since then, land devoted to wildlife has increased from 17,000 to 30,000 square kilometres.

9. Ownership at the communal or private level, rather than by the State, will ensure that the benefits, not just the costs, of conservation will fall on the local population.

10. The sustainable utilisation or CAMPFIRE project in Zimbabwe has brought custodianship of wildlife to the local level - it is a model for future conservation.

IEA Studies on the Environment No. 2

Institute of Economic Affairs
2 Lord North Street
London SW1P 3LB

Telephone: (0171) 799 3745
Facsimile: (0171) 799 2137

£7.50 inc. p+p

ISBN 0-255 36342-7

Down to Earth
A Contrarian View of Environmental Problems
MATT RIDLEY

1. World population growth is decelerating; food, oil and copper are all cheaper and more abundant than ever before.

2. Global temperatures may actually be falling, according to satellite sensors.

3. The ozone layer is getting thicker, not thinner, over temperate latitudes.

4. Winter sown corn, not pesticide use, is responsible for the decline in songbirds on farmland.

5. Some scientists say 20 per cent of species will be extinct in 30 years, yet the actual extinction rate of birds and mammals is 0·00008 per cent a year.

6. Big-game hunters are the best hope for the survival of Africa's wildlife outside a few well-financed national parks.

7. Environmental lobbying organisations are spending more money on lawyers and marketing men to grow their own budgets and less on naturalists and volunteers.

8. Forty per cent of all trees in Britain belong to the government, whose record of mismanagement of forest ecology, public access and finance is second to none.

9. Government conservation schemes are too defensive; their sole aim is to protect rich habitats rather than to improve impoverished ones.

10. Exaggeration, nationalisation and central planning are the enemies of the environment, not the allies.

IEA Studies on the Environment No. 3

Institute of Economic Affairs
2 Lord North Street
London SW1P 3LB

Telephone: (0171) 799 3745
Facsimile: (0171) 799 2137

£8.50 inc. p+p

ISBN 0-255 36345-1